THE

WINDOW GARDENER.

BY

Sprague

EDWARD S. RAND, JR.,

AUTHOR OF "FLOWERS FOR THE PARLOR AND GARDEN," "BULBS,"
"GARDEN FLOWERS," "RHODODENDRONS,"
ETC., ETC.

NEW YORK:
PUBLISHED BY HURD AND HOUGHTON.
Cambridge: The Riverside Press.
1876.

PREFACE TO NEW EDITION.

THE present edition of the "Window Gardener" has been thoroughly revised and greatly enlarged.

Every year has given us many new plants, and some have proved admirably adapted to parlor culture.

These have received notice, and directions for their cultivation have been given.

A chapter has been added on the Culture of Orchids in the Parlor. These beautiful plants, the *élite* of the floral kingdom, are yearly becoming more common ; and as their wants become understood we find that their culture presents no special difficulty. A few years ago it would have seemed impossible to grow orchids in the parlor, yet some species do well.

and doubtless experience will enlarge the number. The culture of Succulents as window plants, to which they are well adapted, and the decoration of vestibules and halls with half-hardy Evergreens, has demanded a chapter, and it is hoped the lists given will prove useful. Many subjects have necessarily been briefly treated, but the author hopes the volume may be found to contain all necessary instructions for window gardening.

GLEN RIDGE, *January*, 1876.

INTRODUCTION.

·As some misapprehensions have arisen, and false statements have been made in regard to the present volume, it is not out of place to preface the present edition with a few words of introduction.

The volume is not wholly a new book, but is mostly composed of a revision of chapters which originally appeared in "Flowers for the Parlor and Garden." The latter work, however, embraces a large range of subjects, many of which are only of interest to those who have extensive horticultural facilities; and this, in addition to its cost, necessarily places it above the reach of the large number who have only opportunities for window gardening, and who only wish a cheap manual of culture.

It was to meet this demand that the volume was originally issued; and the cordial reception it has thus far met in the sale of former editions well attests that it supplies a popular want.

While generally the subject-matter is not new, all has been revised, and the whole volume brought up to the point of horticultural progress of the present year. This, of course, involved the necessity for many changes, and called for the addition of much new matter.

The book is strictly what its name implies, — a manual of "Window Gardening," and contains all the information necessary for the culture of plants in the parlor.

It is not an expensive book, but is a manual of culture for the many; and its price places it within the reach of all who wish to brighten the dark days of winter by the presence of flowers in the window, or who enjoy the home-culture of the pet geraniums, the monthly roses, or the dark-leaved ivy, which often, under the constant care of loving hands, thrive better in the chamber-window than in the costly greenhouse.

The present volume is but one of a series of cheap works on different horticultural subjects; another of which ("Popular Flowers") is already before the public, and of which others are in preparation.

GLEN RIDGE, May, 1873.

CONTENTS.

(7)

CHAPTER I.

WINDOW GARDENING.

Growth of Plants. — Situation and Exposure. — Heat. — Moisture. — Temperature of Room. — Ventilation. — Washing. — Syringing. — Watering. —Choice of Pots. — Window Flower Tables. — Window Shelves. —

(1)

Potting. — Manuring. — Soil. — Peat. — Loam. — Sand. — Leaf Mould. —
— Manure. — Proportions of Each. — Insects. — Green Fly. — Mealy
Bug. — Scale. — Red Spider. — Pruning.

TO grow plants to perfection in a room is not an easy thing. To insure any degree of success, a careful and constant attention to details is necessary. These details are all little things in themselves; they seem almost trivial; but their observance is imperative, if we would have our plants in healthy foliage and profuse bloom. It is by the neglect of all, or some of these, that plants grown in rooms usually present such a diseased, unhealthy appearance.

Any one of us can call to mind some friend, who, as we say, is always successful with flowers; has blossoms when no one else can, and whose plants are models of health and beauty. We laughingly say, the flowers are his friends; he knows them, and they bloom for him; and so it is, in fact; he knows their peculiarities, attends to their wants, feeds them properly, affords the requisite light and air. Is it then a wonder that for him the grateful flowers put on their richest dress of green, and reach out their perfumed blossoms ?

But before we give rules for growing window plants, let us look at these little things, which may come under the head of general instructions. And, first, the

SITUATION.

We have decided to grow window plants, and we must now choose our window. Let it, if possible, face the east or south; that is, be one which receives the full rays of the morning sun. If 'we are unfortunate enough not to have such a window, choose the one having the most sun; the afternoon sun is better than none at all. There are very few plants which will flourish without sunlight, and, as a general rule, the more we can obtain the better. If you have a bay window, looking south, you need ask nothing better.

HEATING.

If possible, choose a room where the temperature at night never falls below forty to forty-five degrees. Let this heat be maintained by an open fire, or by an air-tight stove, on which a large pan of water should be constantly evaporating. A furnace is injurious to plants, by reason of its dry heat only; the little gas escaping from our best furnaces is not sufficient to affect plants injuriously. And while speaking of gas, if possible avoid the use of gas light in the room; the unconsumed gas, always given off, is fatal to delicate plants, and hurtful to the most hardy. If you must use gas in the room, arrange glass doors to shut off your plants from the room, or give up window plants, and confine yourself to growth in Wardian cases. If a furnace is your only means of heating, provide for sufficient moisture by constant evaporation. Another objection to a furnace is, that it keeps the room too warm for a healthy growth of the plants.

The cause of so many window plants showing long, white, leafless stalks, with a tuft of leaves on the end, is, too great heat and too little light. Proportion the two, and you obtain a short, stocky, healthy growth. In rooms, this proportion is always unequal. In winter, there are eight hours of sun to sixteen of darkness; we keep the plant at a temperature of sixty to seventy degrees all the twenty-four. In a green-house, on the contrary, the temperature falls to forty degrees at night, rising, by the heat of the sun, by day, to a maximum of seventy.

VENTILATION.

This must not be neglected; it is as essential to the health of the plant as to the human organization. The best method of providing it is to open the top of the window when the sun's rays are hottest on the plants. The quantity of air to be given must be proportioned to the outside temperature. In cold, cloudy days, but little, and often none, should be given. Care must be taken never to allow a direct stream of cold air to blow upon any plant.

WASHING.

This must be done frequently. A plant breathes like an animal, and not through one mouth, but thousands. As is well known, the plant draws up its food from the soil through the roots, in a liquid form. This food, very much diluted, must be concentrated, and thus assimilated to the plant. We have in the leaves of the plant, a most beautiful arrangement to answer this need. They are filled with " stomata," or breathing pores, which allow exhalation when moisture is freely supplied, and check it when the supply falls off. These little mouths are found on both sides of the leaf in most plants, but usually on the lower side in by far the greater number. They vary in different plants from several hundred to more than one hundred and fifty thousand to a square inch of leaf. Now we are careful in our own persons to bathe daily, lest, as we say, the pores of the skin become obstructed; yet we are willing to allow our plants to go unwashed for a whole winter, when the pores are much smaller, more numerous and delicate, than those of the body. The rule is obvious: wash the leaves of the plants, both under and upper sides, at least once a week; if oftener, the better. Use water moderately warm, and if the plants become very dirty, a little weak soap-suds is beneficial. This washing should be carefully done with a soft sponge or cloth in the case of plants with thick, polished leaves, such as camellias, oranges, and daphnes, Where plants have hairy leaves, or the substance is soft, water is best applied with a small syringe, fitted with a very fine " rose." To use this, place the plant on its side in the kitchen sink, syringe it well, turning it from side to side. Let it stand a few minutes for the water to drain off, and return it to its place: it will thank you for its bath by its bright foliage, Never wet the flowers of a plant; water always injures them; nor allow drops of water to stand on any leaves in the sunshine: the rays of the sun form a focus in the drop of water and scorch the leaf. Once a month, at least, wash the stem and branches of all the hard-wooded plants with a soft sponge dipped in lukewarm water; this prevents the lodgment of insects, and contributes to the health of the plant.

WATERING

Is one of the most difficult subjects to prescribe by rule, yet there are some rules of general application.

Let it be always done with a watering-pot with a fine rose, such as may be procured at any tinman's. The advantage of this is, it allows the water to fall drop by drop over the whole surface of the soil, whereas, if a pitcher is used, the plants are deluged, or holes made in the earth by the stream of water, and the roots not unfrequently disturbed.

Let it be done regularly; the morning is the best time, and once a day.

The surface of the soil should never be allowed to become perfectly dry, nor should it be sodden with moisture. The temperature of the water used is of vital importance. It should neither be cold nor warm, but just the temperature of the atmosphere of the room. Thus no check, or chill, or undue excitement is given to the roots, both roots and branches being equally warm.

A good plan is, to set over night a large pan of water among your flowers, then you will be sure of a sufficiency of water of the proper temperature for the morning watering. If this is too much trouble, remember in watering, it is better to have the water too warm than too cold, that is, of a higher rather than a lower temperature than the roots and branches. Now as to the quantity of water. No rule of universal application can be prescribed. What is life to one class of plants is death to another. The amount of water necessary to make a calla lily thrive would kill a cactus or a heath, and yet the drought necessary for the cactus would be death to the heath.

A good rule, however, is never to allow the soil to become dusty or muddy, and with drainage in potting the latter is easily prevented; by regular waterings, the former. Particulars of treatment for different plants will be given when treating of each plant.

Never allow water to stand in the saucers of the pots unless the plants are semi-aquatic.

Pots.

Choose the common flower-pots, selecting those which are light colored rather than those which are brick red; the former are soft baked and are more porous; in these, the plants thrive better.

Discard all glazed, china, glass, or fancy painted pots; they are not porous, and plants seldom thrive in them. There is nothing neater than the common earthen pot, if kept clean. If, however, something more ornamental is desired, choose some of the fancy pots, — and some are very pretty and artistic in design, — and let them be large enough to set the common pot inside.

But there is a very pretty way of fitting up a window which is but little practised; it is, in fact, making the window a flower garden. Build from your window into the room a rounding wooden shelf, say, if the window is large, three feet in diameter from window to outer edge, but at any rate proportioned to the size of the window. On this, place a large box, wood, or earthen ware unglazed, made to conform to the shelf, and in this put your plants, the taller at the back, the smaller in front, and on each side a climber to run over the top of the window, on a neat wire trellis or on strings.

It is desirable to have holes in the bottom of the box to allow superflous water to escape, and to permit this, the shelf should be covered with zinc, which is preferable to tin, as it does not rust, and have a low rim all around it, with a little hole to drain off the superfluous water running from the boxes. This is a very pretty way of window gardening, but is only to be practised in a very light room; for in a room with but one window, the plants would all grow to the light, and being planted out, they could not be turned as if in pots. A pretty way to grow low plants, bulbs, and is to fit a box, say eighteen inches wide, and as long as the window, into the window, and then place the taller plants behind in pots. This box could be turned as occasion required, or as the plants grew towards the light, or could even be removed from window to window.

POTTING.

But a few words are necessary. Always fill the lower inch of the pot with broken potsherds to secure drainage. In filling the soil around the plants, press it in firmly and establish the plant well. There is no advantage in loose potting.

In re-potting, pare off as much of the old, sour soil as possible, being careful not to injure the roots, and place the ball of the plant in the centre of the new pot, filling in all around with fresh soil. As a general rule, plants need re-potting whenever the roots begin to curl round the inside of the pot, or as gardeners say, " touch the pot." This is easily ascertained by turning the pot down, striking the rim gently against some object by a quick rap, holding the ball of earth and the plant on the palm of the other hand. The plant may thus be taken from the pot and examined, returned again, settled by a smart stroke of the bottom of the pot on the table, and will be none the worse for the inspection. This is also a good way to detect worms in pots, they generally living near the outside of the ball. The operation must, however, be quickly done, or the worm will be too nimble and withdraw into the interior of the ball.

Stirring the surface of the soil is very beneficial, especially for roses, if the roots are not thereby injured. Top dressing is also productive of good effects, particularly with old plants in heavy pots and tubs. It is simply removing the top soil as far down as the upper roots, and refilling the pot with fresh, light, rich soil.

Manuring

Is not generally needed in pot plants. A mixture of powdered or small bits of charcoal in the soil adds a deeper lustre to the green of the foliage and brilliancy to the color of the flowers. Bone shavings produce the same effect on hyacinths.

Liquid manure should be sparingly used, and then very weak.

If guano, a tea-spoonful to a quart of water applied once a week.

Liquid stable manure in about the same proportion, applied as seldom.

Soil.

In potting window plants rich soil should generally be used. The different kinds of soil are, —

Peat, which is black earth or decomposed vegetable fibre, usually taken from meadows or damp woods. If a mixture of white sand is with it, it becomes more valuable.

Loam, our common garden soil. It may be black or light brown. The best is obtained by taking the turf of old pastures and letting it lay till it all crumbles.

Sand, common, or "silver," such as used by glass makers. It should be free from salt. White beach sand may be freshened by frequent washings.

Leaf mould, the decomposed leaves, being the top soil in old woods.

Manure, the material of an old hot-bed, well rotted and entirely decomposed; the older the better.

From these five earths all the soil for green-house operations is compounded.

In treating of each plant hereafter we will give its congenial soil.

As a general soil for potting plants, we would say two parts leaf mould, one part manure, one half part loam, one half part peat, one part sand.

INSECTS.

The only ones troubling house plants are, the green fly, the mealy bug, the scale, and the red spider.

Green fly is to be killed by a smoking with tobacco. Put the plant under a barrel with smoking tobacco; let it remain, say fifteen minutes; then give it a syringing.

Mealy bug is to be searched for and destroyed. Frequent spongings do much to keep down this pest.

Scale is to be treated in the same way. Warm soap-suds are peculiarly distasteful to the creature.

Red spider, which is seldom found on house plants, is nourished by a dry, warm atmosphere. Water is certain death. Keep the foliage syringed and atmosphere moist, and you will have no red spider.

Pruning

Is but little required. Should a branch grow out of place or die, it should be neatly cut off; and a judicious pinching does much to regulate the shape of a plant. Of course all dead leaves and old blossoms should be cut off at once.

'LL teach thee miracles! Walk on this heath,
And say to the neglected flower, "Look up,
And be thou beautiful!" If thou hast faith,
It will obey thy word.

CHAPTER II.

PLANTS FOR WINDOW GARDENING.

(15)

Description. — Potting. — Culture. — Pruning. — Varieties. THE HEATH : History. — Soil. — Drainage. — Watering. — Hard and Soft Wooded. — Temperature. — Summer Culture. — Re-potting. — Insects. — Rooting Plants. — Varieties. THE CYCLAMEN : Potting. — Soil. — Growth. — Seedlings. — Varieties.

N the selection of our plants, we must be much influenced by the extent and location of our accommodations. Some plants thrive with less heat and light than others. As a general rule, choose only green-house plants, avoiding any usually catalogued by nurserymen as stove plants. Discard ferns and lycopodia. With but few exceptions, these perish in the hot, dry, dusty air of our rooms. The Wardian case is their proper place. Remember it is better to grow one plant well than two badly. Because you have roses, geraniums, and daphnes, which do well, it is no reason you should also grow verbenas, fuchsias, and azaleas; your space is sufficient for the first three only; then be content, and do not crowd your plants.

Now let us first give in detail, with their treatment, a list of plants suitable for window gardening; then select those for peculiar exposures.

THE CAMELLIA

The camellia is a native of China or Japan, from whence it was introduced to British gardens about the year 1739. The name was given in honor of Father Kamel, a Moravian priest, whose name, Latinized, became Camellus.

· The plants first introduced were fairly killed by kindness; an error not unfrequently repeated in our day with newly-discovered plants. They were planted in a stove, where the extreme heat soon dried the leaves and parched the plant. We find no further mention of the plant till 1792, when the single red variety (Camellia Japonica) was introduced, and flowered profusely in a common greenhouse; during the next year many plants of this variety were obtained from China; next we find mention of the double red; soon after, the fringed double white, and many varieties too numerous to mention. Strange to say, the single white was not imported till about the year 1820, and even now it is not common, though a showy and free-blooming variety.

The camellia, in its native country, is a shrub or small tree, though Mr. Fortune mentions specimens of the single red as sometimes exceeding twenty feet in height, with

2

trunks of proportionate size. This variety is almost hardy, and in the Middle States will often endure the winter; we have known it to survive even our climate, when well protected.; all other varieties are more tender, and few will bear any severe frost without injury. Most of the kinds in our green-houses are derived from Camellia Japonica, though other varieties have, we believe, afforded fine seedlings.

CULTURE.

The plants should be grown in light loam, or sandy peat and loam, say three parts loam, two parts leaf mould, one part sandy peat; fill the pots one third full of potsherds, to secure drainage, which is indispensable; if the roots of the plant become sodden, particularly during the season of rest, the health of the plant is gone, and years of care may fail to restore its beauty, or remedy the evil caused by a little carelessness in watering. When in a growing state, you can hardly give too much water, and much good may be derived from frequent sprinklings or syringings; this operation, however, must never be performed in sunny weather. One chief care in the culture of camellias is to keep them perfectly clean; dust upon the foliage not only injures the beauty of the plant, but affects its health. The plants are injured by too much heat; some hold that no artificial heat should be afforded, unless necessary to keep off the frost; but as we wish our camellias to bloom at a season when there is but little else to ornament the house, it is advisable to force them moderately.

A safe rule is, never to allow the temperature to fall below forty degrees at night, or rise above sixty-five or seventy degrees during the day. The plants will thus expand the flowers more slowly and naturally, and there will be no complaint of dropping buds, imperfect flowers, and yellow, sickly foliage. One prime mistake in floriculture is the little attention paid to uniformity of temperature; a plant can no more preserve a healthy state when exposed to an atmosphere varying from thirty to one hundred degrees in a few hours, now dry and now surcharged with moisture, than can an animal. The progress of disease may be more gradual, but it is sure to show itself, and, sooner or later, the death of the plant is the result. The plants, when in bloom, should be shaded, as thus the flowers remain in perfection much longer. Give the plants plenty of air at all times, but during the season of growth protect them from chilling draughts, which would cause the young leaves to curl and stunt the plant. During the summer, the plants should be placed in a shady, airy situation, out of doors; allow room enough between the plants for free circulation of air; the practice of setting the plants in a mass, under trees, is most objectionable; in the first place, the drip from the branches overhead is injurious, and again, the pots become filled with earth-worms, which are often difficult to dislodge.

Another mistake in the culture of camellias is too fre-quently re-potting; while the plant should not be allowed to become pot-bound, too much room should not be afforded; a vigorous plant will not require re-potting oftener than every three years; on this point there is, however, some difference of opinion. It is a popular error that the wood of a camellia should not be cut; on the contrary, there is scarcely a hard-wooded plant that bears the knife better; the plant is by nature symmetrical in growth, and, by judicious pruning, perfect specimens may easily be obtained.

Pruning should be done after blooming, just as the plants begin their growth. Not more than one flower bud should be allowed on each terminal shoot, if size and perfection of flower are required; remove all others before the buds begin to swell; if delayed longer, little advantage is gained.

The florists' varieties of the camellia are too numerous to mention; the principal colors are red, white, and rose, with all the intermediate shades. The Chinese profess to possess a yellow variety, but we believe it has never been imported; we have seen a variety named "yellow," the flowers being semi-double, and of a dirty white color.

The following are all well-proved kinds, and may easily be procured of any nurseryman. In buying plants, select those of shrubby form, dark green foliage, without any places where leaves have been dropped; look well to see that the plant is free from scale, red spider, or mealy bug; if possible, examine the roots, to ascertain if they are in a healthy state.

White. Alba plena, Candidissima, Myrtifolia alba, Imbricata alba, Fimbriata, and Oleifera.

Rose, Rosy Pink, or Carmine. Saccoi, Henri Favre, Imbricata rubra, Marchioness of Exeter, Binneyii, Fultonii, Fordii, Floyii, Jeffersonii, Landrethii, Myrtifolia, Prattii, Wilderii.

Blush. Lady Hume's blush, Towne's blush, Pomponia.

White, striped with Red or Rose. Feastii, Eclipse, Duchess of Orleans, Mrs. Abby Wilder.

Red, striped or marked with White. Carswelliana, Chandleri, Donckelaarii, Queen Victoria, Elegans, Elphingstonia.

Crimson. Bealii, Elata, Eximia, Lowii, Palmer's perfection, Sarah Frost, Wardii.

For Seedlings. Waratah, or Anemoneflora, Tricolor, Donckelaarii, Simplex alba, Carnea.

Could we have but one camellia, we would choose
Double white or Candidissima, for white; for blush, Lady
Hume's blush; for crimson, Sarah Frost.

All these are peculiarly adapted for the window.

ORANGE AND LEMON TREES.

These are favorites for parlor culture, and easily grown.
Their treatment is almost identical with that required for
the camellia: the same soil, the same temperature, and the
same general treatment will produce success in the culture
of both.

But they are by no means so clean plants as the camellia,
being very subject to scale and mealy bug. The only
remedy is constant washing, both of the stem and leaves,
with a weak soap-suds warm, and applied with a soft cloth.
Grown in large tubs they do well in a parlor if kept sufficiently cool, and in summer succeed well out of doors.

They are thirsty plants and require much water: good
drainage is essential. From December to March they will
make but little growth; then water moderately. About
the first of March growth begins, succeeded by bloom; then
give more water. After the young growth becomes hard-
ened, they may be set out of doors if the weather is favor-

able. A violent wind disfigures the foliage. The young fruit will set in April and May, and will continue green all summer, coloring the next spring, and holding on the tree a long time. At the first approach of frost, the plants should be removed to their winter quarters. The lemon does not bloom and fruit as early as the orange, and is of taller growth and less fitted for the parlor : the blossoms are smaller and purplish outside.

The little dwarf " Otaheite orange " is a very common variety; and is always noticeable for its profusion of fruit. The flowers are not as fine as the other kinds, though plentifully produced.   The fruit is sweet, but without flavor.

The Mandarin orange is one of the finest species (dwarf), and producing an abundance of fruit of the most exquisite flavor. Unfortunately it is not common.

There are many other larger growing species, all of which produce a profusion of white flowers, exquisitely fragrant.

Among these, the myrtle leaved is conspicuous for its shining foliage, and the large shaddock for its enormous white flowers. The former is as symmetrical in its growth as the latter is tall and ungainly.

Oranges and lemons raised from seed must attain a large size before they will bloom. The better plan is to graft or rather bud the seedling when about a year old. This operation is simple, but is best performed in a green-house, and it is therefore better to employ some neighboring florist to do it. Any variety may be budded on a common seedling stock.

Oranges and lemons will live under neglect, but to grow and flower them to perfection, attention to details, especially of cleanliness, is indispensable.

THE DAPHNE.

This plant, of which the species are numerous, never receives the care and attention its beauty merits. Every green-house contains plants of the well-known *Daphne odorata*, sometimes called *D. Indica* and vulgarly known as " Daphne odora." It is to this plant we intend more particularly to confine our attention.

It is a green-house evergreen shrub, attaining the height of about four feet, remarkable for its long, dark, glossy, green leaves, and its terminal bunches of fragrant, white flowers. It is one of the few old-fashioned plants which the modern rage for novelties has not driven entirely out of cultivation. It has only been thrust into the corners, and left to make its merits known by its beauty and fragrance.

It is one of our most popular flowers, and as a window plant is unsurpassed, flourishing and blooming in situations where most plants would dwindle and die.

With gardeners it is no favorite, because, as they say, it is too straggling, and does not form a neat plant. In some respects this assertion is true, for it is impossible to bring into good shape a plant of this variety when once neglected; but by beginning with a young, healthy plant, much may be done, and fine specimens formed. Let it be remembered that the daphne "breaks" easily. Prune the plant to a bare stump, and in a few weeks buds will start from all the younger wood; therefore prune severely; never allow a branch to remain where it is not wanted, let it be as vigorous or luxuriant as it may, and never be afraid of pruning for fear of losing the flowers.

The cultivation of the green-house varieties of this plant is almost identical with that of the camellia; the same temperature will do for both.

The plants should have plenty of pot room, and the pots be well drained.

Potting should generally be done in the fall, about the time the plants are housed, when as much of the old soil should be removed as possible without disturbing the roots.

The principal varieties are : —

Daphne odorata, the most valuable variety from its season of flowering, which is from December to March, according to the degree of heat given; leaves oblong, lanceolate, smooth; flowers white or pinkish, in terminal heads, produced in great profusion. Introduced from China about A. D. 1770. Propagated by cuttings with great ease. It is one of the best parlor plants we know of, and may be obtained at any green-house at a very trifling expense.

D. odorata rubra is a superior, and by no means common variety; buds, red; flowers, rosy red, with a powerful spicy fragrance. It is a somewhat stronger grower than the last.

There is also a variety with variegated foliage, which is no less desirable, though rather scarce.

Daphne hybrida is a pretty evergreen shrub, hardy in England, but too tender to endure our winters without protection; flowers purple, produced in terminal heads and in lateral bunches very freely, and possessing an agreeable fragrance. It blooms at all seasons of the year, but especially from January to April.

The soil should be four parts loam, two of leaf mould, and one of sand.

THE AZALEA.

The *Azalea Indica*, or Chinese Azalea, is of Asiatic origin. The varieties are innumerable; but the most common and longest known variety is that from which others are but hybrids, *Azalea Indica*.

It is a strong growing plant, with long, coarse, evergreen leaves, producing in clusters of three or more, at the end of the branches red flowers marked with dark spots. This plant may be grown in great perfection, and, as well as all the varieties, is admirably adapted for a window plant. The habit is shrubby, and the flowers are produced in great profusion. *A. Indica alba* has white flowers, and is a fine old variety. *A. Indica purpurea* is a variety with blossoms of a light purple color ; a profuse bloomer, and of rapid growth. There is also a double variety. *A. Indica coccinea* is bright scarlet. From these all the fine varieties of the green-houses have been produced.

To grow the plants in perfection good drainage is essential. Fill the pot one quarter full of broken potsherds, then fill the soil to within half an inch of the top; soil, a dark peat three parts, one part of loam, one half part of silver sand.

Frequent re-potting conduces to the health of the plants. As a general rule, re-pot when the roots run among the crocks at the bottom of the pot. Do not sift the soil; break it into small pieces.

Frequent syringing is beneficial, but over-watering must be carefully avoided. Give full sunshine to the plant, but lay a little moss over the pot if the sun is very hot, to protect the roots.

Keep the plant about the temperature prescribed for camellias.

As soon as the flowers fall growth begins. Give plenty of air and sun, for on this growth depends the bloom of the next year. It should be short, close, and the flower buds be set at the end of each branch.

Set the plants out of doors in the summer, as prescribed for camellias.

Azaleas may be pruned into any shape. This operation should be performed after the flowers have dropped, or after the plant has made its season's growth.

The Azalea is subject to rottenness of the roots, produced by a sodden soil, the effect of over-watering. The remedy is simple: re-pot the plant, and water moderately. Excessive dryness, the other extreme, produces yellow leaves and a general unhealthy appearance.

The following varieties are of proved excellence, and very distinct. All will succeed in the house.

Azalea amœna, a lovely variety; flowers double purple; produced in great profusion in midwinter.

Indica lateritia, salmon; *Danielsiana*, bright red; *Perreyana*, scarlet; *Murreyana*, rose; *Indica alba*, white: *Purpurea*, purple; *Coccinea*, red.

Iveryana, pink and white; *Variegata*, rose and white; *Bledstanesii*, white, striped with red.

This list might be increased an hundred fold.

THE ERICA. HEATH.

All the plants belonging to this genus are of a low, shrubby habit, with fine acicular foliage. None are natives of America. The fine varieties of our green-houses, with the exception of the common *Erica Mediterranea*, are natives of the Cape of Good Hope, whence the gardener's term, " Cape Heaths."

The erica will not thrive unless the soil is adapted to its peculiar nature; this is often very difficult to learn, and experience must sometimes be the teacher. The soil to obtain is one of a friable nature, full of vegetable fibre. We find in an old magazine the best directions we remember to have met in regard to choice of soil. We give them entire for the benefit of our readers : —

" Heaths, like the azalea and rhododendron, make very small, hair-like roots; and where these latter are growing naturally, will be found a good locality to collect soil for the artificial cultivation of the former. This soil will be found full of decaying organic matter. Take up a handful of it, and you will find a mass of thickly grown, fine fibre, feeling like a bunch of moss. Examine it, and you will see that it is chiefly composed of a black debris of leaves and sticks, thickly interwoven with the roots of surrounding vegetation. An inch or two only of the surface should be taken : all below that is generally inferior, the organic matter in it being too much decomposed.

" Where this deposit cannot be obtained, a good substitute will be found in turves from old pasture, cut thin, collected in dry weather, and piled in a heap two or three months before using, so that the vegetation in it may be slightly decomposed. Both in its chemical and mechanical properties such a soil is nearly all that can be wished. In preparing it, however, it is better to chop it up rather fine, securing a proper mechanical texture by the admixture of coarse sand, broken charcoal, or even a few pebbles, or broken potsherds may be used to advantage for keeping the soil open, to allow free admission for atmospheric gases; an essential point to be kept in view in the cultivation of all plants, more particularly those in pots, for they are then entirely dependent on the cultivator for those conditions which they receive in their natural habitats.

" Such a soil as here recommended, kept sufficiently open by any of the above mentioned ingredients, is easily pene-trated by air, thereby increasing its temperature and facili-tating the decomposition of organic matter, during which process various healthful gases are supplied to plants."

In either of the kinds of soil prepared as directed, heaths · will do well. The great point to obtain is a loose, porous soil; for this reason the soil should always be broken, never sifted.

Another requisite in heath culture, is good drainage; this cannot be too strongly insisted upon; with the best of soil, the plants will suffer if water stagnates around the roots.

Fill the pot one fourth full of crocks, and be careful the hole at the bottom is kept open. Never place the pot in a saucer or vessel of any kind, for all water not absorbed must be allowed to drain off. The pots should be clean and free from mould or dirt; cleanliness is a point too much neglected.

In some sections of our country, much difficulty is experienced in growing heaths; the water containing salts in solution which are fatal to the plant, and we know nurserymen who have altogether abandoned their culture. This seems the case in limestone countries, and we have noticed that heaths, of the tender varieties, when watered with "hard" water, grew sickly and soon died. The best plan is to use only rain water, and pursuing this course no difficulty will be experienced. It is a curious fact, that in its native countries, the heath is never found in a soil of which the substratum is lime or chalk. In England, heaths are always grown apart from other plants; with us they occupy the coolest part of the green-house. As a general rule, nothing short of frost is too cold for them, and some varieties will bear several degrees of frost without injury. In the wild state, they are distributed over a vast range of country, which accounts for the different temperatures the varieties require; the degree of cold adapted to each, must be the lesson of experience. Among gardeners, heaths are termed hard-wooded or soft-wooded; the former make only a short growth each season, for example, *E. Cavendishii;*

the latter grow a foot or more, as *E. Caffra* and others.
The two kinds require somewhat different treatment; the
former being far more difficult to manage; they are, however, far more beautiful, some even dazzling from the brilliancy of their flowers. Heaths require plenty of air. If
crowded, they are subject to mildew; a disease much more
easily prevented than cured. Air should be given, if possible, every day; but cold draughts should be avoided during the growing season.

Though heaths are often lost during the winter by growing them in too high a temperature, yet the greatest mor-
tality is caused by the heat of summer. With many it is
the custom to treat the plants as other hard-wooded plants;
to turn them out doors during the summer, under the shade
of some tree. The consequence is, the pots are often
exposed to the hot sun, the tender fibrous roots become
parched, and the plant dies; or else the drip from the trees
rots the roots, producing the like result. Our experience
has shown the best plan to be a different treatment for the
plants according to their age. Early in June, all young
plants should be planted out in a bed with a northern
exposure; there they will grow luxuriantly during the summer. Before the September frosts, re-pot them with care,

3

and winter as old plants. We have found a large bed prepared for rhododendrons and azaleas the most favorable
place. It is sheltered from the south by a belt of white
pines. The soil of prepared peat is suited to the wants of
the plant, while the large foliage of the rhododendrons
keeps the soil moist by preventing rapid evaporation. For
the older plants, we choose a shaded spot, and prepare a
bed of coal ashes; slope the bottom to carry off superfluous
moisture; plunge the pots in the bed of ashes, and if the bed
is exposed to the sun for any length of time, shade by an
awning. Be careful not to crowd the plants; a free circulation of air is essential. By this mode, the pots are never
exposed to the rays of the sun; the plants receive plenty of
light without being burned, and by syringing at evening,
and sprinkling (not pouring) water upon the pots and bed,
a sufficiency of moisture is secured. Some varieties of the
soft-wooded class, such as Caffra rubra and alba, margaritacea, and others, do best planted out in the full sunshine.
The growth becomes short and stout, and the plants are
more hardy and less liable to injury. By this course, however, all beauty of foliage is lost, for the plants become of a
rusty brown color, which never disappears till the leaves fall.

. Re-potting should be done whenever the roots become

matted or collected at the bottom or sides of the pot; examine to see if they are healthy; if so, give them a larger pot; if not, prune off those which are dead, remove the old soil, and pot in the same size, or smaller, as the case may require.

The custom with gardeners is to pot heaths in the spring, but the grower must be guided by the state of the plant.

Insects give but little trouble, where proper regard is paid to the plants.

Mealy-bug is sometimes found; the best course to pursue, if the plant is badly infested, is to throw it away, for it is almost impossible to remove the insect; if but slightly affected, pick them off, and wash the plant well with warm soap-suds; whale oil soap is preferable. The same rules apply when the plants are troubled with black or brown scale. *Erica arborea* is particularly subject to attacks of the former, and from the fine, close nature of its foliage, it is very difficult to clean.

We have never known our heaths to be troubled by red spider or by aphis.

In growing ericas, some attention must be paid to pruning, or rather to pinching; the plants should never be allowed to grow tall and spindling; they should be grown near the glass, and, by frequent turning, prevented from becoming one-sided. Some varieties are of symmetrical form by nature; others require much care to control the too luxuriant branches.

Heaths strike freely from cuttings. Take the tops of the young shoots, about an inch in length; prepare a pot or pan of heath soil; cover this with silver sand to the depth of half an inch; insert the cuttings about half their length, as thickly as you please; cover them with a glass, and frequently wipe the moisture from the inner surface of the glass; keep them slightly moist, and shelter from the direct rays of the sun.

When rooted, pot off the cuttings into small pots filled with heath soil, with the addition of a little more sand than is used for the old plants; as soon as the season permits, plant them out to make growth. In re-potting plants or cuttings, care should be taken never to sink the crown of the root lower than it was before; rather raise than sink it.

There is no plant which makes a greater show, or proves more attractive as a specimen, than the erica. In England, it is grown in the greatest perfection, some of the plants being twelve feet high, and eight feet in thickness. Can a more superb object than such a plant be imagined, when in full bloom?

From over five hundred varieties, we cannot be expected to give all that are deserving of cultivation; as before remarked, none are destitute of beauty. The periods of bloom are from January to November; indeed, we may have heaths in bloom every month in the year. The following list contains a select variety in colors: —

White or Light-Flowered. Arborea, Margaritacea, Grandinosa, Bow-ieana, Jasminiflora, Conferta, Vestita alba, Odorata, Ventricosa, Pellucida, Wilmoriana, Caffra alba.

Red Flowers. Gracilis, Ignescens, Mediterranea, Caffra rubra.

Scarlet or Crimson. Ardens, Cerinthoides, Hartnelli, Splendens, Coccinea, Vestita fulgida, Tricolor.

Purple Flowers. Amœna, Mammosa, Melanthera mutabilis, Propendens tubiflora.

Lilac. Baccans, Suavolens.

Yellow. Cavendishii, Depressa, Denticulata.

Green-Flowered. Gelida, Viridiflora, Viridis.

For window culture, the varieties succeeding best are Caffra rubra and alba, Margaritacea, Arborea, and Mediterranea.

We have been thus diffuse in treating of this plant, because it is a general favorite, yet never seen in good condition in the parlor.

The plant is very hardy, yet impatient of the least neglect. A single day's omission to water, or a drenching, with poor drainage, will kill the plant; yet it will languish for months, and all your care will fail to restore it. If the hair-like roots once become parched or sodden, the plant will die.

We do not recommend it for a window plant, yet its beauty is worth all the care required; and will not some be fired by ambition to make the heath a window plant?

THE CYCLAMEN.

This pretty flower is too little known. It is a native of Europe and Asia, some varieties being very abundant in Switzerland and Italy, and is to be found in almost every green-house. It is of the easiest culture. Pot about the latter part of November, in a rich loam, with a dash of silver sand; an addition of about a spoonful of the old soot from a flue will increase the size and brilliancy of the flowers. It must be well incorporated with the soil. Bits of charcoal, broken fine, serve the same purpose. Place the crown of the bulb just above the surface of the soil. The size of the pot must be determined by the size of the bulb; as a general rule, cyclamen do not require large pots.

Good drainage is indispensable. Keep the plants cool till the leaves are well grown, always keeping them near the glass. When the flower buds begin to rise on the foot stalks, remove to a sunny shelf, where they will soon show bloom. By shading, the duration of the flowers is prolonged. When the bloom is past, gradually withhold water; the leaves will turn yellow, and the plants should be kept dry, in a state of rest, all summer. Do not allow the plants to ripen seed (which they do freely) unless you desire seedlings, to increase your stock. The seed germinates easily, sown in rich loam, and seedlings bloom the third year. Some find difficulty in preventing the shrivelling of the bulbs during the summer. Our best cultivators, to prevent this, bury the bulbs during the summer in the open border; take them up about the middle of September, when they are found fresh, plump, and in good condition for a start. There is one risk, however, in this method: mice are very fond of the bulbs, and sometimes commit great havoc. There is shown in this plant a curious provision of Nature: no sooner has the flower faded, than the stem begins to curl up, and buries the seed capsule in the ground, at the root of the plant; this is designed to protect the seed from birds, and to sow it in a congenial soil.

. Good-sized, blooming bulbs may be obtained at any green-house, for from fifty cents to one dollar each for the more common varieties. This bulb is particularly adapted for window culture, and will give more flowers, with less trouble, and occupying less space, than any flower we are acquainted with. The more common varieties are *C. Persicum*, white, tipped with rich, rosy purple; *C. Persicum album*, pure white; *C. punctatum*, resembling Persicum. All these flower from January to March. *C. Europæum*, pinkish purple; *C. Europæum album*, pure white; *C. hederafolium*, very large, rosy purple, a splendid variety. All these bloom from October to January.

Bright gems of earth, in which perchance we see
What Eden was, what Paradise may be.

CHAPTER III.

PLANTS FOR WINDOW GARDENING.

THE GERANIUM. THE PELARGONIUM: History. — Culture. — Soil. — Potting. — Winter Treatment. — Varieties. THE VERBENA: History. —
Culture. — Cuttings. — Summer Culture. — Potting for Winter. — Watering. — Soil. — Seedlings. — Properties of a good Verbena. — Window
Culture. — Varieties. THE HELIOTROPE: History. — Culture. — Pruning. — Varieties. THE SALVIA, OR MEXICAN SAGE: Summer Culture.

(41)

THE GERANIUM.

NDER this head, we propose to treat of the plants usually known, in common parlance, as Geraniums, including both those horticulturally and botanically known as such, and Pelargoniums. Between these there are many minute and fanciful distinctions, which are only interesting to botanists, and need not concern the amateur. The true geraniums are herbaceous. For window gardening, their treatment must be the same.

For the pelargoniums, we are chiefly indebted to the Cape of Good Hope; the geranium is found, in some of its varieties, in Asia, Europe, and America; two of the family, our "wild geraniums," being familiar to us all as among the wild flowers of spring.

The scarlet, or horse-shoe geranium, so called from the color of its flowers, and the dark marking of its leaves, is a very common and popular window plant. The rose, oak,

8 *

and nutmeg geraniums are commonly grown for their fragrant leaves, and for their hardiness, as they can endure more hard usage than most plants.

The general fault in geranium culture is, crowding. The plants need light and air on all sides, and unless this is afforded they soon become one-sided, long-drawn, and straggling, with but few leaves, and these in a tuft at the end. The blossoms are small and few, and the whole plant presents a picture of vegetation under difficulties.

The fine varieties of pelargonium, called "Fancies" by florists, it is useless to attempt to grow to any perfection in the house. They need constant care; and the rules for growing them as specimens, laid down by English florists, are sufficiently confusing and contradictory to involve the amateur in a maze of difficulty.

Light, air, and cleanliness are the three primary rules for growing geraniums. The horse-shoe and high-scented varieties are not troubled by insects. The pelargoniums (large-flowered geraniums), require constant attention to keep them free from the green fly, which increases upon them with wonderful rapidity. If the weather is warm, and the plants at all affected by the fly, they should be smoked once in ten days, and frequently syringed. Surely the beauty of

the flowers will compensate for any trouble. To prevent
" drawing," that is, the growing of the plants towards the
light, all geraniums should be frequently turned, which will
give a well-proportioned plant. If the plants grow too tall,
pinch out the top; all the axillary buds will then break
into lateral branches. Again, if the side branches become
too close, prune them out fearlessly. The geranium breaks
easily, and you need never be afraid of killing the plant,
even if you prune it down to a bare stump.

Soil.

Pelargoniums and geraniums require a strong soil; that
is, good sound loam, such as will grow melons. The top
of a pasture will answer well. Let it be carted home and
laid up in a long ridge, so as to expose as large a surface to
the air as possible. Keep it clear of weeds, and let it be
turned over every little while. To two parts of this loam,
add one part of two-year-old cow dung, well turned over.
Old hot-bed dung will do nearly, but not quite as well.
Then add about one part of river sand and bits of charcoal,
mixed. Let all these ingredients be kept in separate heaps
till wanted for potting, then mix them in the above proportions, and use them moderately dry. This compost should

be used to bloom and grow the plants in. For the winter season, use a small quantity of leaf mould instead of dung. Fresh soil is always to be preferred, for old soil is apt to become cloddy and sour.

POTTING.

All being ready, put the drainage in a suitable sized pot. Place first a suitable crock, or a large oyster shell over the hole; then lay a few large crocks upon that, and smaller upon those, so that the drainage may occupy about three fourths of an inch. Place a thin layer of moss upon the drainage, and upon that a sprinkling of soot or charcoal dust; after that a thin layer of the rougher parts of the compost, and finally a layer of soil. Then turn the plant out of the old pot, pick out the old drainage, and loosen part of the old roots, spreading them over the new soil as much as possible. Then see that the collar of the roots is just below the rim of the pot, and fill in around the ball with the fresh soil, pressing it down gently as it is put in. When the pot is full, give it a smart stroke or two upon the bench to settle the soil; level it neatly, leaving it about half an inch below the rim of the pot. This finishes the potting. Then give a good watering of tepid water.

For four or five weeks, while new roots are running into the fresh soil, they will not need a large supply of water; but when the roots reach the sides of the pots, and the leaves and shoots are advancing in growth, then water will be required in abundance.

They should never be allowed to flag.

After a hot, sunny day, let the plants, in addition to the water at the roots, have a gentle syringing. Exercise discretion, however, on this point.

The geranium is a spring and summer blooming plant. It is very difficult to obtain a flower from December to April; therefore, during the winter it should be kept cool, and moderately dry.

About the first of February re-pot the plants, give more heat, sun, and water, and your plants will bloom profusely in May.

The varieties grown only for their leaves may have more generous culture during the winter months.

VARIETIES.

Ivy-leaved geranium (*P. lateripes*), is a pretty trailing species, with ivy-shaped leaves and purple flowers in the summer. There is also a variety with white flowers. It is a pretty window plant, and always does well. It needs plenty of light, sun, and generous culture.

The varieties of horse-shoe geraniums (*P. zonale hybrids*), are all good window flowers, and will often bloom in winter. The following are the best old varieties : —

Scarlet. Dazzle, Tom Thumb, Defiance.
Cerise. Cerise unique.
Pink. Rosa mundi.
White. Boule de Neige, Lady Turner.
Variegated Leaved. Flower of the Day, Golden Chain, Alma, Bijou.

These latter varieties need a green-house to develop the rich colors of the foliage, yet they do well as bedding plants in the summer.

P. graveolens is the common rose geranium.

THE VERBENA.

There are few plants which lend more beauty to the flower garden in summer, or enliven the green-house in the winter and early spring months in a greater degree, than the verbena. From the variety of colors, the rapidity of propagation, the little care needed to bloom the plant in per-fection, and the abundance of blossoms, it is, and always must remain, a universal favorite.

In addition to these advantages, the facility with which new varieties are raised from seed, render it a favorite with the amateur; and in no collection do we fail to find the verbena, in some of its many varieties.

It is a difficult task to prescribe the culture of a plant so well known, and which will grow and flourish under such a variety of circumstances, and in such different situations. As every one has grown verbenas, each has his own peculiar mode of treatment, if, indeed, a flower requiring so little care can be said to have peculiar treatment.

In writing of a plant, from which seedlings are produced with such ease, and which sports into such an infinite variety of colors and shades, we cannot be too careful in expressing a decided opinion. Every year new seedlings are "brought out," and latterly the varieties have so multiplied that it is very difficult to choose those really worthy of cultivation : the favorite of this spring may, after a year's trial, be cast aside as worthless, for it may not be found worthy of general cultivation, or better varieties may have been originated.

Our verbena was introduced into England from Buenos Ayres, where it is indigenous, by Mr. Hugh Cumming, an ardent lover of nature, about the year 1825.

The first, and for a long time the only variety cultivated, was *Verbena melindres*, or *chamœdrifolia;* but it now appears lost among the new and superior kinds which have been raised from seed. In form, it has been repeatedly excelled, but its creeping habit and abundance of bloom must always recommend it, though we doubt if at the present time it can be obtained at any of our green-houses, and probably few of our younger cultivators have ever seen this once popular variety. The color is scarlet, and though perhaps equalled, can never be excelled. Many other earlier varieties might be mentioned, but, although interesting, it would too much extend the limits of this article.

Verbena multifida, with lilac purple flowers, was introduced from Peru; *Verbena Tweediana*, with rose crimson flowers, from Brazil; and from these, and a few other varieties and seedlings, have sprung all the numerous varieties, many hundred in number, which may be found in extensive collections. The credit of introducing this plant into the United States belongs to Robert Buist, of Philadelphia. About the year 1835, from seed received from Buenos Ayres, he raised the first white, pink, and crimson verbenas. The plant soon became generally known, and was every where a favorite; in the floral world it caused

4

quite an excitement, and the original kinds were soon sur-
passed, in every respect, by newer seminal varieties.

The culture of the verbena is very simple. The plants
will bloom with very little care, but to grow them in perfection requires attention; of thousands of plants of any size,
scarcely one is a fine specimen. Let us, beginning in early
spring, trace the plant, as generally grown, and then see
how much a little care might increase its beauty.

About the first of February, cuttings of the young shoots
are taken from old plants: in a sandy loam, a few weeks,
and sometimes a few days, will suffice to root them; they
are then potted off into thumb pots, and, if placed near the
glass, will soon show a terminal flower. As soon as the
season is sufficiently advanced, these young plants are bed-
ded out, and, in favorable seasons, soon form a conspicuous
feature in the flower garden, continuing to bloom till long
after the early frosts. About the first or middle of September, the gardener begins to re-pot his plants for winter, and
the common practice is to take a runner, which has rooted
well at a joint, and, after suitable pruning, to pot it for
winter blooming and propagation. Others, again, take up
the old roots, while others, by sinking pots in their verbena
bed, about midsummer, allowed the runners to root directly

in the pots; the pots being taken up, and the connection with the mother plant cut, the young plant receives no injury or check. But this mode is very objectionable, for two reasons: first, the loam in the pots is apt to become sour and sodden; and again, earthworms often enter the pots, and prove injurious during the winter. The plants are housed, and, for a long time, produce no flowers, and are any thing but ornamental. Soon after the new year, they begin to grow vigorously, but are allowed to trail carelessly over the staging, or droop from some hanging shelf. No care or attention is bestowed upon them, except to give the daily supply of water.

The days grow towards spring. Cuttings are again taken off; the same process is repeated year after year; and thus one of our loveliest flowers, which, with a little care, might be one of the greatest attractions and ornaments of our green-houses, is never seen in perfection, except in the garden.

That this is the fact, is to be deplored; yet the remedy is simple. By beginning about midsummer, we may have verbenas in bloom as well during the winter as the spring months. About the first of August, or earlier, cuttings should be taken from desirable varieties. In a fortnight they will be ready to transplant. Pot them in thumb pots, and re-pot as soon as the roots touch the sides of the pot. Keep them in vigorous growth by affording plenty of light and air, being careful they never suffer from want of water. Pinch off the leading shoots, to cause all axillary buds to break, and in no case allow them to bloom. Train the plant in any form desired, but be careful not to permit it to grow too straggling. When other plants are housed, remove your verbenas to some warm shelf, where they may have the morning sun, and on every favorable day give plenty of air, and fumigate well to destroy green aphis. Your plants will soon be in luxuriant bloom, long before those potted in the common way have shown a bud, and will continue to afford an abundance of flowers until late in the spring. To grow verbenas well in the house in summer is far easier. They may be bloomed in pots of any size, and trained in almost any form, the only requisites being plenty of light and air, careful pruning, and means to destroy aphis and keep off mildew.

One great fault in growing verbenas is the practice of watering too copiously. The plant, as originally found, grows on dry hills; and damp not only produces mildew, but rots the roots, and thus destroys or produces disease in the plant.

The proper soil for verbenas, is two parts of loam, two of leaf mould, with an admixture of sand, and in this we have found them grow and bloom luxuriantly.

Many verbenas, which for green-house blooming are unsurpassed, are worthless for bedding purposes; the petal of the flower being too thin, or the color fading or changing. Again, some bloom well in winter, others far better in summer; some form large masses and flower well, others are of rambling growth and poor bloomers; some of creeping, others of more upright habit; while a few possess every desirable quality; and in making a selection, all these properties are to be considered.

We have said that seedlings were produced with great ease. The verbena seeds well where the plants have not been too long propagated by cuttings. A long-continued propagation by cuttings seems to diminish the power of the plants to produce seed, and, as a general rule, the further removed a plant is from a seedling, the less the chance of its perfecting good seed. The seeds may be sown in a hot-bed or green-house, early in spring, and the plants, when about an inch and a half high, pricked out in the border; it is a good plan to pinch out the leading shoot, as thus the plants branch and become stronger; the plants grow rapidly, and soon show bloom.

But to raise a seedling is one thing, to raise a fine seedling, a far different. Of many hundred raised in the course of the last few years, by the writer, not more than half a dozen have been worthy of preservation, and only one (and that produced by chance) really a first-class flower.

In raising seed, much may be done to insure its quality by planting fine varieties together, and allowing them to intertwine, then gathering the seed from these plants. No rule can be laid down to obtain any desired color, for the seedlings sport infinitely. We can only approximate towards definite results; thus, if we plant Annie (white) and Robinson's Defiance (red) together, the seedling will be likely to be pink.

The flowers of the verbena are of every color and shade, except light blue, which color has never been obtained. A good yellow verbena has not yet been produced. There is a miserable variety, with a small truss of dirty yellow flowers. The writer, some years since, by a curious process of watering and fertilization with a white verbena, obtained a seedling, which proved, on blooming, to be of a light straw color; the plant was weak and sickly, and died before cuttings could be taken. Since that time he has tried the experiment often, but never with any successful result.

The qualities of a first-class verbena, as laid down by florists, are : roundness of flower, without indenture, notch, or serrature; petals thick, flat, bright and smooth; the plant should be compact, with short, strong joints, either distinctly of a shrubby habit, or a close, ground creeper or climber; the trusses of bloom, compact, standing out from the foliage, the flowers meeting, but not crowding each other; the foliage should be short, broad, bright, and enough to hide the stalk; in the eyed and striped varieties, the colors should be well defined and lasting, never running into each other, or changing in the sun.

As a window plant, there is nothing that will give more bloom than a verbena. Let it be trained on a trellis, and give it all the sun possible; the more sun, the more bloom. Pinch the shoots, to prevent its becoming too rambling, and give air enough, and your work is done.

The production of seedlings, as above directed, is a very pretty amusement, and very simple. Seedlings will bloom in three months, from the seed.

Verbenas may be grown to advantage in the garden, either in masses, as single plants, or upon rock-work; many pretty effects may be produced by a careful arrangement of colors; they are also well adapted for hanging pots and for vases, in which they will bloom profusely.

There is no flower which, if properly grown, will better repay the care required, and none which will show so well with but little attention, and we trust that these few remarks may lead to a more careful cultivation of this beautiful plant.

THE HELIOTROPE.

This plant is always admired for its fragrance, and will ever be a favorite for window culture.

It is a native of Peru, and has been in our gardens since the year 1757.

The details of culture are similar to those prescribed for the verbena; the soil should be strong loam, with a little sand and manure.

The heliotrope is seldom grown as well as it should be. It should have frequent re-pottings, and be allowed to grow large. We have seen them in parlors, in large tubs on wheels, and eight feet high. Such plants are in themselves bouquets of beauty, being always covered with flowers. Train the main stems of the plant to a trellis, and let the branches droop naturally, and as they will gracefully. The plant bears the knife well, and breaks freely, so it can be trained into any shape.

The common variety is *H. corymbosum*, then the oldest, *H. Peruvianum; H. Volterianum* is a fine dark variety, but not so strong growing.

Florists' catalogues contain many varieties, but the above are the best for general culture.

THE SALVIA.

This plant is only valuable as a window plant in summer and early autumn. The chief variety cultivated is the Scarlet Mexican Sage (*S. splendens*), introduced from Mexico about forty years ago. It is a rank growing shrub, with long, jointed stalks, crowned with rich, scarlet flowers. The best way to grow it is to set the plant in rich soil in the garden in spring. It will grow vigorously. About the last of September pot it (it transplants easily), shade it for a few days, then remove it to a sunny window, where it will delight you with its brilliant blossoms for two months. Then keep it cool until spring, and repeat the operation until the plant becomes so large as to be unmanageable; then spring cuttings must be taken off and rooted.

The proper soil is, three parts loam, one leaf mould, one manure, with a sprinkling of sand.

Salvia patens is an exquisite blue flowered variety. It blooms well in the garden in summer, and the fleshy roots may be preserved like a dahlia through the winter.

There are many other fine varieties.

THE TROPÆOLUM.

This flower, from its earliest discovery and introduction, has been a popular favorite. As year by year newer varieties have been discovered, or finer seedlings raised from old favorites, it has steadily advanced in favor, till now, the rich man's choicest green-house and the poor man's garden alike boast some of the varieties of this beautiful plant. In the limits of a short article, like the present, it will be impossible, of course, to give a detailed description, or even to mention all the varieties; many are only desirable in a collection, being of inferior beauty; while others are rare, or of difficult culture, and therefore found only in the green-houses of amateurs.

The different varieties of tropæolum divide themselves into three distinct classes. First, those with bulbous, or rather tuberous roots, such as *Tropæolum azureum* and others. Second, those with large, round leaves, and large showy, often coarse, flowers, as the various varieties of *Tropæolum majus*. Third, those with small, delicate, regularly-formed flowers, with smaller leaves, and more of climbing rather than trailing habit, such as *T. Lobbianum*. We are aware that this division is imperfect; that some varieties partake of the characteristics of more than one class, and that others are with difficulty included in any of the three; and to any one acquainted with all the different varieties, the difficulty of classification will be at once apparent. We shall, therefore, only attempt this general division; leaving a particular description to be given when we treat of each variety. The soil to be used in the culture of the tropæolum is, for the bulbous varieties, leaf-mould and peat, with an admixture of fine sand; for the other classes, an addition of more sand is to be advised, as care must be taken not to enrich the soil too highly, for in a rich soil, with plenty of room to develop the roots, the plants are apt to run all to leaves. This may be prevented in two ways, either by giving a poor soil, or by allowing the roots to become "pot-bound," and nourishing the plant by slight waterings of liquid manure; they generally fail to give satisfaction if the soil is close, heavy, and binding. All the varieties, we believe, are readily propagated by cuttings, and many produce seed in abundance. Some succeed better if allowed to trail on the ground; others are so delicate as to need constant attention and careful training. Some are hardy in England, though to our knowledge none have ever been able to survive our severe winters in the open ground, or protected in frames. All the varieties are of the most rapid growth, and are mostly free flowerers; none are destitute of some beauty, while the greater number are remarkable for the combinations of dazzling colors which they afford. The prevailing color is yellow in its different shades; next, red; then dark; and lastly, a most extraordinary fact, which puzzled the botanists, a beautiful blue. It had been asserted and argued, with great show of reason, that a flower, of which all the known varieties, or the general types, were of red, yellow, or cognate colors, could, by no possibility, be found related to a plant with blue flowers, or could there be a blue flowering plant in the same class. The discovery of a blue tropæolum, in 1844, completely refuted this theory. In the treatment of the tropæolum, it is essential for the good health of the plants that they should enjoy plenty of light and air; without this, they cannot fail to become sickly or unsightly from faded leaves and small flowers.   A supply of water should be given with the syringe, overhead, occasionally, which will conduce to the vigor of the plant, and destroy the red spider, which sometimes attacks the leaves.   The plant, in all its varieties, is remarkably free from disease or insects; we have occasionally had the more delicate varieties troubled by green fly, and by mealy bug, but very little care will prevent this. The chief danger seems to lie in the decaying of the roots by over-watering when in growth, or by not withholding water when they are in a state of rest.   These remarks, of course, apply only to the bulbous varieties.   Sometimes we have known the roots of the summer-blooming varieties to be attacked by the root aphis, but this is unfrequent.   The foliage is of too fiery a taste to be subject to the attacks of insects.

With these few remarks we will proceed to the description of the different varieties, noting any peculiarity in the habits of each, or any peculiar mode of culture which may be best adapted to its nature.

The oldest and best known variety is TROPÆOLUM MAJUS, the common nasturtium of our gardens — a native of Peru, but very early introduced.   This occurs in a variety of colors, and under a variety of names.   The colors are chiefly red, yellow, very dark, and all the intermediate shades; or, again, red upon yellow in spots, shadings, stripes, or bands, or yellow upon red or dark ground. Scarce two flowers, unless self-colored, will be found alike, and there is no prettier sight than a flower bed filled with this variety, the various colored flowers contrasting finely with the large round leaves. At any seed store, varieties may be obtained; and by a little care in planting the seeds, a beautiful effect may be produced. This species is of the easiest culture, and will grow almost without care; it is well adapted for covering rock-work, or any unsightly spot, producing from the latter part of June until killed by the frost, a constant succession of brilliant flowers and ornamental foliage. All the varieties of this species are annual, and are propagated either by seeds, which are freely produced, or by cuttings of half-ripened wood, which root freely in sand.

TROPÆOLUM MAJUS ATROSANGUINEUM is only a very fine variety, as its name implies, of the above. It was introduced into England as early as the year 1684. The required soil is light and rich; it flowers freely; increased by seeds and cuttings.

It would be useless to attempt a description of the

varieties of *Tropœolum majus;* so constantly do they
change, that each year, as newer seedlings are produced,
the older are forgotten and lost. All are well worthy of
cultivation, and some of the varieties should be in every
garden. We have seen a double variety, but it was evi-
dently a mere sport, which was only propagated and preserved as a curiosity in a collection; the colors were con-
fused, and the blossom destitute of beauty.

We pass now to the varieties of *Tropœolum minus,* being
those comprised in our last class, and seemingly only
reduced specimens of *Tropœolum majus.* We have seen it
stated that this variety was introduced before *Tropœolum
majus,* but we believe the best authorities agree on the
latter being the oldest known variety. Be this as it may,
both were known in Europe at a very early period. The
plants of *Tropœolum minus,* and its varieties, may always
be distinguished from those of *Tropœolum majus,* and its
varieties, by the leaves; in the former, the nerves of the
leaves always end in a point, which is never the case with
those of the latter.

TROPÆOLUM LOBBIANUM, sometimes called *T. peltopho-
rum.* One of the very finest; first collected by Mr. Lobb,
in Columbia. A rampant grower, and free flowerer in the

green-house; color of flowers, orange scarlet. The temperature of the house to bloom it well, should be kept about fifty degrees; a slight watering of liquid manure should occasionally be given. It does not succeed well with us in the open border; our summers are too short, and the plants are apt to be nipped by the frost just as they are fully set with flower buds; it strikes freely from cuttings, and produces seed sparingly. Most of our fine, new varieties are probably hybrids between this and the following.

TROPÆOLUM PULCHERRIMUM. Like the last, a rampant grower; color of flowers, bright yellow, with starry rays of orange scarlet at the base of the petal; a free flowerer in the green-house. Culture like the last.

TROPÆOLUM SMITHII. A brilliant red variety, a native of the high mountains of Columbia; treat as *T. majus;* will bloom well in the open border.

TROPÆOLUM RANDII. A very fine seedling· of Mr. Joseph Breck's; a very vigorous grower; the writer has, in one summer, had one side of a large green-house covered by a small plant. This variety has the desirable property of blooming equally well as a border plant in the summer and in the green-house in winter. The color of the flower is brilliant yellow; the base of each petal marked with a round black spot; the flowers are often veined with purplish red, sometimes very deeply, and, from a large plant, often dozens of blossoms, all of different shades, may be gathered; this is particularly the case in the green-house; in the border, the colors are more constant. This is probably from its abundant flowers and free habit, the most popular variety of its color, among gardeners for bouquet purposes, and, though of comparatively recent introduction, is very widely disseminated. Propagated by cuttings; produces seed sparingly.

TROPÆOLUM PERIGRINUM, ADUNCUM, or CANARIENSE, commonly known as canary-bird flower. A very lovely and popular variety; grows about ten feet high, and blooms well if the soil is not too rich. It is commonly cultivated as a summer border plant, but will bloom well in the green-house. To this end, plants should be struck during the summer, and grown with plenty of light and air; let the soil be loam, and well rotted manure, with a little sand; do not give the roots too much pot room, and water occasionally with liquid manure. Plants may also be raised from seed, but they flower less freely than those struck from cuttings. This lovely variety is too well known to need description.

5

We have been thus diffuse in treating of this plant, because it is the best climbing window plant we have. Give it sun, and it will be a mass of bloom all winter. A pretty way is to train it up the side and across the window on strings. Do not, however, give it a very large pot, or it will all run to leaves. It should also have a sandy soil.

. . . . All Eden bright,
With these, her holy offspring, creations of the light;
As though some gentle angel, commissioned love to bear,
Had wandered o'er the greensward, and left her footprints
there.

CHAPTER IV.

PLANTS FOR WINDOW GARDENING, CONTINUED.

Roses. China Rose: History. — Description. — Soil. — Pruning. — Watering. — Varieties. Tea Rose: History. — Culture. — Varieties. Bourbon Roses: History. — Culture. — Varieties. Pinks: Indian Pink. — Carnation. — Difference between Carnation and Picotee. — Classes. — Soil. — Potting. — Care of Flowers. — Culture out of doors. — Prop-

(67)

N continuing our list of plants adapted for window gardening, we come
to the queen of flowers, the Rose.
A book, rather than a portion of
a chapter, should be devoted to this
flower; but as our space is limited, we must
with a word, dismiss the large divisions of
June, Hardy or Hybrid Perpetuals, Pro-
vence, Damask, Galic, Moss, Climbing, Austrian,
Noisette, and Banksian Roses, each of which would require
a separate treatise, and confine ourselves to the China,
Bourbon, and Tea families.

Many of the others are of great value for the green-
house, some being, in our climate, purely green-house
roses, and others being invaluable for forcing; but none
succeed with parlor culture, though many are well known
in the garden, and may claim more than a passing mention
when we come to the concluding portion of our book,
the Flower Garden and Shrubbery.

CHINA ROSE.

And, first, the China rose. While treating of parentage, we may also include the tea rose, which, with the China, comes from the same ancestor, the *Rosa Indica* and its varieties. From this stock come all the China and tea-scented roses, which, by skilful hybridization, are now so multiplied that already their name is legion. Properly speaking, the three roses which are the oldest, and may be considered parents of the race, are *Rosa Indica*, the common Chinese rose, *R. semperflorens*, the crimson or sanguinea rose, and *R. odorata*, the Chinese or sweet-scented tea rose.

The China rose and its hybrids are usually stout growing, and sometimes of a close, twiggy habit. With us they will not endure the winter without protection, but south of Baltimore, stand out uninjured.

They are the common rose of window gardening, and are known as "monthly roses." The colors vary from white to deep crimson or red, running through all the shades of blush and pink.

They are often exposed for sale in early spring at the corners of streets and in the market places, every little shoot being crowned with a bud or flower. The foliage is generally smooth, glossy, and fine cut, clothing every little twig, and of a lively, fresh appearance.

It will survive almost any treatment, and will live if but a ray of sunlight can reach it. It is the poor man's friend, and clings to him in every vicissitude; yet, while possessing adaptability to circumstances in a remarkable degree, no plant will better repay care and attention. Cleanliness, washing, and syringing are essential to good health; give plenty of light, and it will repay you by abundance of bloom. Though as its common names (daily or monthly rose) imply, it will not *bloom* every day, yet there will seldom be a day when it will not have a flower or a bud upon it. It will ask you, too, for an occasional smoking; for the green fly is very fond of the delicate juices of its young shoots, and this indeed of all roses.

Do not give it too large a pot. Roses will do well in smaller pots, in proportion to their size, than almost any other plant.

Soil.

Yet the soil must be rich and well mixed. It should consist of four parts of the richest black loam, or leaf mould, two parts of well-rotted manure, with a slight admixture of fine sand. This soil should not be sifted, but lumpy, yet well mixed together.

In potting, as much of the old soil as can be taken off without breaking the roots, should be removed, and the plant set just up to the neck or collar, on the new soil; settle the earth well around the plant, and give a gentle watering from the fine rose of a watering pot. Pruning should be done as required; the eyes will break any where; therefore, whenever a branch becomes too long or unsightly, cut it in; there need be no fear of injuring the plant.

If they have been planted out in the garden during the summer, on removal to the house in the autumn they will need a severe pruning. Cut off the young wood to within a few inches of the old wood, and give the plants a little rest, by giving less water and little heat; when you wish them to bloom, bring them into full sunlight, give more heat, and, as soon as the young branches have begun to push, give plenty of water. Every eye will produce a shoot, crowned with one or more buds; after blooming, shorten in the blooming branches about one half; new eyes will push, and a second display of bloom be the result. In watering roses, care must be taken not to render the soil cold and sodden; water should never stand round the roots; frequent stirring of the surface of the soil is very beneficial. A few bits of charcoal, broken fine and mixed with the earth, will impart the richest brilliancy to the flowers.

The following list of China roses will be found to include the best old varieties. New hybrids are constantly produced, and all of this class make good window plants. China roses are called also " Bengal " roses.

List of China Roses.

1. *Agrippina,* or *Cramoisi Superieur.* Rich, velvety crimson, very double.

2. *La Superbe.* Purple crimson, very double, flowers always opening well.

3. *Eels Blush.* A profuse bloomer; flowers large and double, resembling a tea rose.

4. *Indica,* or *Common Daily.* Dark blush or rose color; free grower and profuse bloomer. This is the common "monthly rose."

5. *Indica Alba.* A white variety of the last, of more slender growth, but double and free flowering.

6. A dwarf form of *R. Indica,* called " *Fairy Rose,*" *Tom Thumb, Lawr.n.eana,* is a pretty little miniature rose, very double, and about as large as a dime or half dime.

7. *Mrs. Bousanquet.* Creamy blush, very fine; by some classed as a Bourbon, which it seems to be. It is very distinct from other Chinas.

8. *Semperflorens,* or " *Sanguinea.*" Very double, cupped; rich crimson. Every where grown and appreciated.

9. *Jacksonia.* Bright red, very double.

10. *Louis Philippe.* Dark crimson; globular.

11. *Eugene Hardy.* White, changing to blush.

12. *Eugene Beauharnais.* Bright amaranth, very fine form, and fragrant.

There are many others which may be found in florists' catalogues.

F r one rose for bloom, choose No. 8 ; for two, Nos. 8 and 3 ; for three, Nos. 8, 3, and 12 ; for four, add No. 4 ; for five, add No. 2 ; for six, No. 9 or 1.

TEA ROSES.

The original rose (*R. odorata*) was only introduced about 1812, and from this have sprung our many fine varieties. The treatment required is identical with that of the China rose ; yet a richer soil, and more heat and light, may be afforded to advantage. The former is easily done by increasing the proportion of manure in potting.

They also need more care, and are not so patient under neglect. For summer bedding in the garden, they are unsurpassed. Usually their growth is more delicate and graceful than that of the China varieties.

The following list includes some of the best varieties, which may be relied upon for window or garden growth.

They will not bear our winters unprotected. This list may be multiplied fourfold from catalogues: —

1. *Adam.* Bright pink; large and cupped.
2. *Comte de Paris.* Creamy rose; large and fine.
3. *Caroline.* Bright, rosy pink or flesh-colored; large and very fine.
4. *Gloire de Dijon.* Yellow, shaded with salmon and rose; an immense flower; very full; not always opening well with window culture; by some, considered a "Bourbon."
5. *Clara Sylvain.* Pure white; double; very fragrant.
6. *Yellow Tea.* Pale yellow; long, beautiful bud; very fine.
7. *Elise Sauvage.* Bright yellow, fading to white; large and fine.
8. *Madame Desprez.* White; very fragrant.
9. *Safrano.* Fawn color or saffron; sometimes rosy; not very double, but fine in the bud.
10. *Triomphe de Luxembourg.* Buff salmon, shading to rose.
11. *Souvenir d'un Ami.* Rose and salmon; fine.
12. *Goubault Rose.* Yellow centre; large and fine.
13. *Le Pactole.* Lemon yellow; very fine.
14. *Bougère.* Browzy, rosy lilac; a strong grower.
15. *Odorata.* Fine blush, well cupped.
16. *Bon Silene.* Rosy salmon.

For one rose of this class, for window culture, we should select No. 15; then add No. 9, No. 12, No. 14, No. 5, No. 2, No. 1.

BOURBON ROSES.

The union of the Damask Perpetual with the China rose has produced the new and distinct race known as Bourbons. They have a peculiar habit and foliage, are free, vigorous growers, and much hardier than the China rose. In the Middle States, they are perfectly hardy, and will endure our winters with but slight protection. As bedders, they are unsurpassed, and bloom during the whole summer. They are usually wintered in frames, like the China and tea roses. For window gardening, they are not as suitable as those species, yet their beauty renders them worthy of a permanent place, where space can be given, and for greenhouse and conservatory blooming, they are magnificent.

Their treatment is identical with that of the species above described.

The following are fine varieties: —

Bouquet de Flore. Light, rosy carmine.
Dr. Roque. Purplish crimson.
Gloire de Dijon. See tea roses.
Madame Desprez. See tea roses.
Dupetit Thouars. Bright crimson ; very showy.
Leveson Gower. Deep rose ; very large.
Souvenir de la Malmaison. Pale flesh color, very large and fine.
Queen of Bourbons. Fawn-colored blush ; a free bloomer.
Sir Joseph Paxton. Deep rose ; very fine.
Paul Joseph. Purplish violet.
Hermosa. Light blush or rose color ; very fine form.
George Peabody. Dark, velvety crimson.
Mrs. Bosanquet. Pale flesh color ; good form ; very fine.

The most satisfactory method of growing roses is to build a small pit for them. Plant them out in a rich soil, and they will bloom summer and winter. Very little heat is required to winter them safely, and the sashes being entirely removed in summer, all the benefit of growth in the open air is obtained. On the approach of frosty nights, the sashes are put on, and the roses bloom all winter.

THE PINK.

Next to the rose, this is a favorite flower, and as a window plant, does equally well in spring and summer.

We shall at once dismiss the garden, Indian, and florists' or Paisley pinks, and confine ourselves to the carnation and picotee, these being the varieties for window culture.

Yet a word for the double crimson Indian pink. It is a pretty little flower, always in bloom, and only needs light and a rich loam to make it a beautiful window plant.

The best way to procure it is to buy seed; sow it in the spring, in the garden, and on the approach of frost, pot the plants for winter blooming. It may then be easily increased by slips or layering.

The carnation pink is a very old inhabitant of our gardens. It is said to have been introduced into cultivation from Italy or Germany before 1510.

The question is often asked, What is the difference between a carnation and a picotee? None, botanically; it is purely a florist's distinction. The carnation has the marks on its petals, from the centre to the edge, in flakes or stripes of colors, on a white ground. The picotee has a white or yellow ground, the edges of the petals being fringed with various shades of red and purple.

Carnations are divided into five classes, namely: 1. Scarlet Bizarres; 2. Pink or Crimson Bizarres; 3. Scarlet Flakes; 4. Rose Flakes; 5. Purple Flakes.

Bizarre is derived from the French, meaning odd or irregular. The flowers in these classes have three colors, which are irregularly placed on each petal. Scarlet Bizarres have that color predominating over the purple or crimson; but the Pink or Crimson Bizarres have more of these colors than the Scarlet. Scarlet Flakes are simple white grounds, with distinct stripes or ribbons of scarlet. Rose and Purple Flakes have these two colors upon a white ground.

Picotees are divided into seven classes: 1. Red, heavy-edged; 2. Red, light-edged; 3. Rose, heavy-edged; 4. Rose, light-edged; 5. Purple, heavy-edged; 6. Purple, light-edged; 7. Yellow ground, without any distinction as to the breadth of the edge color.

Pinks, both picotees and carnations, are of little use as house plants until well into the spring; if however, they are grown, they should be kept cool, and rather dry; there is nothing gained by trying to force them. The best method of growing them is in the open border, preserving them in a cold frame through the winter. If grown in pots, they are much more difficult of management. In the open border, they bloom in June, July, and later, and are an indispensable ornament. We do not recommend the .pink as a window flower, but have been constrained to include it in our list, as it is a favorite flower.

The rules we give are very full, and apply both to the window, the cold frame, and the garden; they are compiled from English authorities, and possess little claim to originality.

PROPAGATION AND GENERAL TREATMENT.

Soil for Culture in Pots. Get the turf from an upland pasture; take off about three inches thick, and keep it in a heap for a year, to cause the grass roots to decay and mellow the soil; chop it, and turn it over four or five times during the year; it will be in finer condition for use. During this, the worms and grubs, especially wire worms, should be picked out, for it is frequently the case that the soil best adapted to the carnation contains its greatest enemy. Before being used, the soil should be passed through a coarse sieve or screen, and the fibre rubbed through with the soil. The soil in which the plants are bloomed, and that in which they are kept in small pots through the winter, should be different, for in the latter they are not required to make much progress, and the less they are excited in autumn and winter the better, provided they make steady progress and preserve their health. This can only be secured by abstaining from the use of stable dung, using pure loam, and such decayed vegetable matter as is afforded by the grass naturally growing in loam when the turves are cut. Neither should the loam be too adhesive, but sufficiently porous to allow the water to percolate freely; should it not be so naturally, a little sand may be used to lighten it. In preparing the soil for blooming the plants, take of this loam three parts, well decomposed leaf mould one part, thoroughly rotted cow dung one part (if this cannot be obtained, hot-bed manure, well decomposed, in fact, reduced to a fine, black mould, may be substituted), and of sandy peat, one part. A small portion of old lime rubbish, slightly sifted, will be of service to the plant, mixed among the compost. Being duly mixed, in sufficient quantity, let it be brought under shelter to dry some time before the potting season.

On receiving the plants from the nursery, if in the fall, they should be potted, as above, in four-inch pots, giving two inches of crocks at the bottom for drainage, and nearly filling the pot with the earth, but highest in the middle, and spreading the roots as much as possible all around alike. The soil is only just to cover the roots, and to be pressed gently to them, and in this state, after watering, to settle the loam about their roots, they should be placed in a common garden frame, upon a hard bottom, into which the waste water, when refreshed, cannot soak, but with a very gentle slope, that any water which runs through the pots may run away. In the winter management, the chief object is, to give all the air they can have in mild weather by taking the lights off; to give them water very seldom, and never till they absolutely want it. If to be grown in pots, they should be re-potted early in twelve-inch pots, two or three plants in a pot, using the soil above directed. Let there be at least three inches drainage. In putting them in those large pots, let the ball of earth be turned out whole, rub off a little of the surface, and, after having filled the large pot high enough with the compost, place the ball so that the collar of the plant, which is just above the surface of the old ball, be within half an inch of the edge of the pot; put the soil around it; press it down between the ball and the side, and fill the whole up level with the collar of the plant and the edge of the pot. Let them all be placed in a sheltered spot, and refreshed with water when they require it; which will be more or less frequently, according as the season be dry or wet. Let each pot have a stake in the centre, to which the plants may be closely tied as they rise up for bloom. When they show their buds, remove all but three, and the flowers will be the finer, and not more than one blooming shoot may be left on each plant. When the buds have swollen, and are about to burst, tie a piece of bass matting round the middle, and carefully open the calyx down to the tie, at all the divisions, as the flower can then open all around alike; otherwise, they frequently burst on one side, and it is then difficult to form an even flower. As the petals develop themselves, they should be shaded from the sun and rain, either of which would damage the flowers. Culture in pots is seldom resorted to in this country, unless it be for exhibition purposes; and it is for the benefit of amateurs, who wish to grow them for that purpose, that we have given such minute directions.

Culture in Beds and the Flower Border. This is the

6

most common method in this country, culture in pots being attended with more trouble, and occupying more time, than can usually be given.

They succeed admirably in any good garden loam, provided it is well drained; wet or moisture, when over abundant, is very injurious. The soil should be trenched to the depth of eighteen inches in the fall, enriching it at the same time with leaf mould and cow's manure, thoroughly rotted; should the soil be heavy, an addition of refuse charcoal, lime rubbish, or sand, will be beneficial, leaving the surface rough, that the frost of winter may act upon it. In the spring, the beds should be again thoroughly spaded to the depth of one foot, and raked smooth; after which the plants should be turned out of the pots, leaving the ball entire, and planted two feet apart each way. The after treatment may be the same as recommended for pot culture.

Propagation. By layers and pipings, for increasing approved sorts, and by seed for the production of new varieties.

By Layers. The time for performing this operation is when the plants are in full bloom, or a little past. The shoots of the plant, around the bottom, should then be brought down to the ground, and, when rooted, separated from their parent. The materials needed for layering are a sharp, small knife, a quantity of notched pegs, and some finely-sifted soil. Choose a dull, cloudy day on which to perform this work; or, if the plants are in pots, they may be layered in any weather. Begin by trimming off the leaves from the bottom of a shoot, leaving the two uppermost on, and entire. Trim off the lower leaves on every shoot before layering one, because, when a layer is tongued, it is easily broken off. When this is done, take hold of the shoot, turn it up, and pass the knife blade through the third joint upward, commencing the cut just below it; then reach a hooked peg, thrust it into the soil, catching hold, by its hook, of the layer as it descends, and press it gently down to the soil. Do the next in the same manner, and so on until every shoot is layered, then cover them all with the sifted mould, about three quarters of an inch deep, and the process is completed; then give a slight watering, and the layers require no further care, but watering, until they are rooted, which will be in about a month or six weeks. When sufficiently rooted, pot them off into five-inch pots, a pair in each; or, if your space is limited, and the layers small, three may be put into each pot. After they are potted, they should be placed under glass, in a cold frame or pit, plenty of air given in mild weather, and shelter from severe frost, when it occurs. Very little water is required during the winter months, and the air in the frames should be as dry as possible. Should damp prevail, the plants, some fine day, should be taken out, and a coat of fine, dry coal ashes spread over the surface. The plants should then be replaced in the pit.

By Pipings. Carnations may be propagated by this mode, where there is the convenience of a gentle hot-bed. It is, however, not so safe as layering; but when there are more shoots than can be layered, and it is desirable to propagate largely, the superfluous shoots may be piped. Cut off the lower part of the shoot, up to the third joint, trim off the lowest pair of leaves, and pass the knife just through the joint. Prepare a pot, by draining it, and filling it with the compost up to within an inch of the top; fill that inch with silver sand, water it gently to make it firm, and then insert the piping all around it, close to the pot sides; place them in a gentle hot-bed, shading from the sun; watch them daily, and supply water when the sand becomes dry. When they are rooted, which they will show by sending up fresh leaves, pot them in pairs, as directed for layers, and treat them in the same manner.

By Seeds. The seeds may be sown, during the spring months, in boxes or pans filled with the same description of soil as before recommended. Let the surface of the soil be made even, and the seed, evenly scattered over it, cover them to the depth of a quarter of an inch with finely sifted mould. If early in the season, the pans may be put in a moderate hot-bed, just to cause the seeds to germinate, but must not be long kept there for fear of weakening and drawing the plants. Without artificial heat, the seeds may be sown in May, placing the pans or boxes in an open, airy part of the garden, but shaded from the sun, at least from ten in the morning till four in the afternoon. Moderate moisture will be indispensable, but if the soil be kept too wet, the plants are liable to damp off, or to be otherwise injured. When the plants have acquired six leaves, and are about two inches high, they should be pricked out in rows six inches apart, keeping them well watered until they have taken fresh root. About the beginning of October, they should be potted for the convenience of wintering. Plant out in the spring, in a bed prepared as before directed. As soon as the blossoms can be seen, all the single sorts should be taken up and thrown away, to give the double ones more room to grow. The finer blossoms ought then to be selected for layering or piping.

The following list comprises a few of the varieties : —·

CARNATIONS.	PICOTEES.
Admiral Curzon,	Esther,
Coriolanus,	Prince Albert,
General Simpson,	Amy Robsart,
King of Carnations,	Haidee,
Falconbridge,	Ophelia,
Acca,	Princess Royal,
Squire Trow,	Lamia,
Valentine,	Duke of Newcastle,
Benedict.	Ganymede.

THE FUCHSIA.

If by a *window plant* we mean one which blooms in winter, then the Fuchsia is not a window plant. A few solitary blooms may be produced during the spring, but the summer is its season of glory.

As a pot plant, for summer blooming, it is unsurpassed, being very floriferous, of brilliant foliage, and symmetrical habit. All of our garden varieties are hybrids, from ancestors introduced from South America and Mexico. Strange to say, there is a New Zealand species also. The first, *F. coccinea*, was introduced from Chili, just before the year 1800.

The plant is of the easiest culture; the growth is rapid, and a young spring cutting will make a large plant by autumn. The secret of growing the plant is, never to let it stop growing until you have it of the desired blooming size; keep re-potting, as soon as the roots touch the pot, until you get it into a twelve-inch pot, which is large enough for the window blooming of a fuchsia. Give plenty of light and air; turn the plant frequently, lest it grow one-sided, and fumigate when needed to kill green fly. The best form to grow a young plant is the pyramidal. Train up a leading shoot, and if the plant is supplied with pot room and plenty of light, and has not heat enough to draw it out weak, it will form side shoots in sufficient abundance to produce a handsome outline, the branches being allowed to take their own pendent form. The plant may also be prettily grown on a flat trellis. The best place for a fuchsia in winter is a dry cellar, free from frost, where they should be kept nearly dry. About the first of March prune back all the side shoots, and leave only the upright stem; prune in the roots also, and re-pot them in as small a pot as will hold the roots; as the eyes break, thin out those which are not needed, leaving enough to give plenty of side branches. Re-pot, and treat as above directed.

SOIL.

One part of peat, one of loam, and one of leaf mould will grow them well; thoroughly mix the component parts, and break it rather fine; be careful to secure good drainage.

VARIETIES.

Every spring gives us a host of new varieties, most of which are discarded in a few years. The white corollaed varieties are generally of weak growth, and not adapted for culture out of the green-house. Those with a double corolla we do not admire; the multiplication of floral leaves detracts much from the simple beauty of the flower; they are, however, valuable in a collection, and very showy.

Fuchsia coccinea is a pretty species, with purple and white sepals and corolla.

Fuchsia serratifolia, a species with scarlet tube, tipped with green, blooming in winter.

There are some twenty other species, which are beautiful in a green-house, but valueless for window growth.

The following hybrid varieties are all fine: —

Venus de Medicis. Tube white, sepals blush white, corolla deep blue; fine habit.

Etoile du Nord. Bright scarlet sepals and tube; corolla black violet, with short, reflexed sepals.

Souvenir de Chiswick. Tube and sepals rosy, crimson, violet; corolla fine.

Ajax. A fine, dark variety.

Empress Eugenie. Crimson sepals, white corolla.

England's Glory. Fine white; scarlet corolla.

Globosa. Scarlet; purple corolla.

Glory. Crimson; violet corolla.

Lady of the Lake. Crimson blush; white corolla.

Mrs. Story. Scarlet sepals; white corolla.

Wonderful. Scarlet tube and sepals; violet corolla.

Queen Victoria, La Crinoline, Omar Pasha, Nil Desperandum, Duchess of Lancaster, Climax, Guiding Star, Rose of Castile, Roi des Blancs, Prince Frederic William, are all fine varieties.

Bring flowers . . . .
They speak of Hope to the fainting heart;
With a voice of promise they come and part.
They sleep in dust through the winter hours ;
They break forth in glory! Bring flowers, bright flowers.

CHAPTER V.

PLANTS FOR WINDOW GARDENING, CONTINUED.

MYRTLE: History. — Soil. — Culture. — Varieties. ACHÆNIA: Ease of growing. — Soil. ABUTILON: Culture. — Soil. — Varieties. THUNBERGIA: Sowing. — Training. — Insects. — Soil. — Varieties. ALOYSIA, OR LEMON VERBENA: Culture. — Soil. — Watering. CALLA: Resting. — Blooming. — Soil. CUPHEA: Culture. — Potting. — Soil. CACTUS: Divisions of the Family. — *Cereus:* Summer Treatment. — Pruning. — Wa-

THE MYRTLE.

YRTLES are natives of Europe, New Holland, and China. They are hardwooded, evergreen shrubs, possessing a peculiar, agreeable fragrance, and have always been favorites for parlor culture.

The soil should be three parts loam, with one part of sand and one of leaf mould.

They do not require very large pots, and flourish well in almost any situation.

They require moderate washing, and watering, and plenty of light and air during the growing season, which is in summer, when they should be put out of doors in a shady place, yet not under the drip of trees. The flowers are usually white, and produced in profusion in midsummer. *M. communis* is the common plant of our parlors, of which there are many varieties, with small and large leaves, variegated foliage, and flowers single or double.

M. tenuifolia is a New Holland species ; a fine plant for parlor culture.

M. tomentosa is a fine Chinese species, with purple flowers changing to white, so that flowers of many shades are seen at once on the same plant. It should be more generally grown, being equally hardy, except it is impatient of exposure to the hot sun.

ACHÆNIA.

A. malvaviscus is a beautiful parlor plant, symmetrical in growth, and producing its brilliant, scarlet flowers in profusion at the end of every branch. These flowers are succeeded by white berries, changing to bright red, which alone would make the plant ornamental did it not always display a profusion of bloom.

The best way to grow the plant is as a pyramid, as thus the flowers and fruit show to great advantage. Give plenty of sun and light, turning the plant frequently. It is not subject to the attacks of insects. Soil, two parts loam, two leaf mould, with a slight admixture of sand.

ABUTILON.

This is a race of shrubby, green-house plants, well adapted for the parlor.

They are free growers, of upright habit, and unless judiciously pruned, will soon outgrow their quarters. They are natives of South America and New Holland.

The proper soil is, two parts loam, two of leaf mould, and one of sand. If the soil is too rich, the growth will be too rapid for the full development of the side branches. Keep the plant moderately moist. The varieties for parlor culture are, —

A. venosum, with large yellow flowers with red veins ; *A. Bedfordianum,* flowers much of the same character.

A. striatum, one of our prettiest window plants ; always in bloom, and beautiful from its profusion of pendulous, veined, red and yellow blossoms all winter.

There are many other varieties, some with white, others with red flowers, but they are not recommended for house plants. The variegated-leaved kinds lose their coloring under window culture.

THUNBERGIA.

These pretty plants are usually grown as annuals with us, for summer decoration in the flower garden, but they also make fine window plants. For this purpose, sow the seed in August in pots; as the plants grow, transplant one to each pot, and train the slender shoots on a neat trellis. Give plenty of sun, and syringe very often, for the plants are very subject to attacks of red spider. They will show bloom about the middle of January, and produce a profusion during the winter and spring months. The plants will show bud very early, but if they are allowed to bloom, growth will stop; therefore it is best to pick off all the flower buds until the plant is of the required size, when they may be allowed to open.

Cuttings root very freely in sand, under a bell glass. The soil should be, one part turfy loam, one part peat, one part well-rotted manure. Water moderately.

The varieties are, —

T. alata, buff yellow, with a black centre; *T. alata aurantia*, deep orange, with black centre; *T. alata alba*, white, with black centre.

There are also some superb hot-house species.

ALOYSIA, OR LEMON VERBENA.

A half-hardy deciduous shrub, from Chili; the only species is *A. citriodora*, commonly called Lemon Verbena. It is valuable only for the fragrance of the leaves, the flowers being small, whitish lilac, and of little beauty.. As a winter plant it is of no value, as it needs a season of rest, which must be given it in a cellar free from frost.

The best treatment is, to plant it out in spring in the flower border, where it will make vigorous growth. In the fall, before the first frost, remove the plant with a ball of earth to the cellar. In spring, trim the plant into a neat shape, and re-plant it. If grown in pots, the proper soil is, two parts of loam, two of leaf mould, and a slight mixture of sand. · While the plants are growing, give plenty of water, but withhold it entirely during the winter.

CALLA.

The only plant of this genus, worthy of cultivation, is the well-known Calla Lily (*Richardia Æthiopica*). It is too familiar to our readers to need description. To bloom the plants well, they should have a season of rest, which may be regulated so as to have bloom at any season, if we have several plants. They naturally rest after the blooming season. When they again begin to grow, re-pot them; if a plant with a single stem is required, remove all suckers, otherwise they will do no harm to remain; but the plant requiring frequent re-pottings, will soon become so large as to be unmanageable.

The foliage is peculiarly fine, and the plant is worth growing for this alone.

If bloom is particularly desired, the best way is to plant some six or eight roots in the half of an oil cask. Paint it green, and put on two iron handles; you thus have a very cheap, pretty, serviceable, and durable tub. Fill this with the richest loam, and set the plants, the largest in the middle, the smaller around the sides, and set the tub on the piazza or in a grass plat. The plants will bloom during the summer very freely, and may be wintered in a light cellar without difficulty.

The proper soil is richest loam and peat well mixed. When growing, you cannot give the plants too much water. In the window, if the plants are set in a saucer kept constantly filled with water, they will be the better for it. In summer, the plant will grow well, and flower profusely out of doors in a tank.

CUPHEA.

The only plant of this family, desirable for a window plant, is the little Mexican *C. ignea* or *platycentra*. This is a sparkling little gem of a plant, always in bloom. Plant it in the flower border in summer, re-pot in autumn, and all winter it will gladden you by a profusion of its bright scarlet tubes tipped with a ring of black and white. The plant never grows above a foot in height, and is just suited for the window. Soil, about three parts loam, one each of sand and manure. Water freely, but do not allow the soil to become sodden.

CACTUS.

There are seven families of Cacti, containing each a great number of species. Those chiefly grown as parlor plants come under the families *Cereus* and *Epiphyllum*. The former family is a native of all dry, tropical regions of the western continent.

The soil most suitable is, two parts peat, one part broken potsherds, broken coarse, one part loam or old mortar rubbish, and one part manure; mix these well together and secure good drainage.

During the summer, the plants should stand out of doors

7

in a sheltered place, from the time they have done flowering until September. Then remove them to the house, all parts of shoots having no bloom buds (they are easily seen along the leaves) being cut back to just beyond the buds. The plants should be confined to six or eight strong stems; while these are in good health, the growth of shoots from the roots is not to be encouraged.

Give the plants no water from September until February; while in growth, water moderately. They bloom from May to August.

Some of the varieties are, —

C. Speciosissimus. Crimson and purple flowers.

C. Flagelliformis: Rose flowers. This variety should be allowed to droop, and not be pruned.

C. Grandiflorus is the night-blooming Cereus; flowers yellowish white. This variety will not bloom until it is old.

C. Maynardi. Deep orange red flowers.

C. Triangularis. Cream color; immense flower.

All varieties will do well as window plants. The first is the best for general culture.

We now come to the latter family, *Epiphyllum,* all natives of tropical America. This branch of the Cactus family is distinguished by flat shoots, and leaves without spines. The soil and treatment is identical with that of the Cereus. The best varieties are, —

E. Akermanni.   Fine scarlet flower.
E. Jenkinsonii.   Fine scarlet flower.
E. Speciosum.   Rosy pink flower.
E. Alatum.   White flower.
E. Truncatum, and its varieties, with scarlet, rosy, red, violet, and white flowers.

All these latter varieties are drooping, and to show to advantage, should be grafted on some of their tall-growing Cereus relations.   *C. speciosissimus* makes the best stock.

HYDRANGEA.

This is only a summer plant, but an old favorite.   One requisite for its successful culture is shade; if grown in the sun, the leaves become browned and the plant does poorly. With us, it is not hardy out doors, so it must be grown in a tub, and wintered in the cellar.   The flowers are produced on the shoots of the previous year.   It requires to be well grown to flower profusely, and the flowers from young plants are larger than those on plants three or four years old.

While growing, the plants should have a good supply of water.

Soil, one part loam, one part manure, one part peat. The color of the flowers is pink, but if iron filings be mixed with the earth they will become blue.

Besides the well known pink variety (*H. hortensis*), there are many others; of these, *H. japonica,* with blue and white flowers, is desirable.

AGAPANTHUS,

Or African Lily. A showy plant for summer blooming, and too well known to need description. Soil, two parts loam, one part manure, one part leaf mould. Well grown it is a noble plant, but will bear much ill-usage. Treated as recommended for the calla lily, and planted in a tub, it forms a fine plant.

Winter in a dry, light cellar, and water occasionally. Water freely while growing.

Ther: is a white variety, and one with variegated foliage; both desirable; a native of the Cape of Good Hope.

OLEANDER.

A very showy, but much neglected plant; too well known to need description. To bloom them in perfection, they need a stove, and yet do well in the parlor and out of doors.

Their season for blooming is July, yet that may be changed, and bloom produced at any season. They flower freely when scarcely a foot high, but will grow to the height of ten or fifteen feet, forming splendid trees covered with rose-colored, white, or variegated flowers.

Give them plenty of pot room in soil, two parts loam, two parts peat, one part well-rotted manure. Being subject to white scale, frequent washings are desirable.

They may be wintered in a light cellar, and then should be but little watered; during the growing and blooming seasons, water should be abundantly supplied.

The principal varieties are double rose (*Nerium oleander splendens*), striata pleno, with double striped flowers, purpurea, dark red, and as many as 'fifty named varieties, all good.

PITTOSPORUM.

This is an old-fashioned plant, a favorite for its fragrant flowers rather than for any beauty of foliage or blossom; the former is dull green, the latter dirty white.

The common variety (*P. Tobira*) is a native of New South Wales, and in England is a hardy wall plant; with us it is a parlor plant, blooming from February to May. Soil, three parts loam, with one each of leaf mould, sand, and manure.

Water freely while in bloom and growth. During the

summer, set the plant in a sheltered situation out of doors.

The leaves need frequent washings, to keep them free from dust.

This plant will thrive with very little sun.

JASMINE.

A family of favorite climbing shrubs, and very pretty for window culture, alike desirable for their neat foliage and fragrant flowers. The flowers are white or yellow, and produced from February to June, or later.

The soil should be equal parts of loam and peat, with a slight admixture of sand. The only insect attacking them is scale, which a little care in washing will soon remove. With common room culture, they grow to a large size and make superb plants.

Water should be rather freely given. They should be trained on neat trellises, and the branches allowed to droop. The most desirable varieties are, —

J. Azoricum. White flowers in summer.
J. Odoratissimum. Yellow flowers in spring.
J. Multiflorum. White flowers in spring.
J. Nuliflorum. Yellow flowers in spring.

CALCEOLARIA.

The best way to grow this pretty plant is by raising seed-lings. Sow seeds in August, in light, rich loam; trans-plant the young plants to separate pots ; pinch out the cen-tre of the plant, and continue to do so until the plant is of the required blooming size. As the roots of the plant touch the pot, re-pot into a size larger. When the flower stems push up, tie them neatly to sticks. Be careful in watering not to give too much, or your plants will damp off. Give all the sun and air possible, and keep the plants as close to the glass as you can.

The proper soil is three parts light, rich loam, one of fine peat, one of sand.

The shrubby varieties are seldom grown as window plants, but are reserved for the flower garden. Under the treatment given above, they grow and bloom well.

MAHERNIA.

This is a lovely flower and a general favorite, always blooming, and always attractive with its fragrant yellow bells.

Its tendency is to grow straggling, therefore it is best to

select a plant with a straight stem. Tie up the main stem as it grows, and by continued pinching restrain the too luxuriant growth

M. odorata is the variety chiefly grown. *M. Hector* and *Diana* are pretty orange and pink varieties.

Soil, four parts loam, one of sand, one of manure. Keep the plants moist, but not wet, and give as much sun as possible. In bloom from February to May.

CHINESE PRIMROSE.

Both the single and double varieties of this plant are pretty for window gardening. Sow the seed in July, in a fine soil, as directed for calceolarias, and treat the plant the same, except the pinching. By January, nice little blooming plants will be formed; give them sun and air and do not allow them to over-bloom, as they are apt to do.

After bloom is over, set them out of doors (about June), and on no account allow them to bloom during the summer. Grow them well until autumn, then re-pot in blooming pots, and by Christmas they will begin to show flower, and keep up a succession until spring.

Soil, one part turfy loam, one part well decomposed cow dung, one part peat, and one part sand.

Be sure the pots are well drained, and never keep the plants very wet. The colors are red, rosy, lilac, white, striped, and mottled, with fringed and plain edges.

SOLANUM.

The only plant of this useful family, suitable for room decoration on account of its flowers, is the *Solanum jasminoides*, a pretty climber, with dark green foliage, and white potato-like flowers, in large clusters.

It is useful to climb around a window or to cover a trellis. It is a rampant grower, subject to no disease or insect attacks, and with sun and air, if potted in a soil of rich loam, will take care of itself, and bloom all winter.

SOLANUM PSEUDOCAPSICUM.

This plant is the common Jerusalem Cherry. It was introduced from Maderia about the year 1596. For a showy plant, in the parlor or green-house, it has no equal, being studded with bright, red berries, about the size of a cherry, during the whole winter. A plant now before us, only two years old, is two feet high, three feet through, and bending down beneath the weight of fruit. The flowers are produced in June, and are inconspicuous. Sow the seeds in a pot in April; as soon as the weather becomes warm, transplant to a rich, sunny border; the plants will grow rapidly, and probably be in fruit the next winter; pot the plants before the frost, and winter in room.

There is a more dwarf-growing species (*S. capiastricum*), with orange berries, which is also very ornamental.

A strong loam is the proper soil for all plants of this family.

THE LAURESTINUS.

This plant, hardy in England, is with us a winter-blooming parlor ornament. It is a free-growing, free-blooming evergreen, and will bear much hard usage. If cared for, however, it will repay the attention. The flowers are small, white, and in large, flattened panicles, expanding from February to May.

The proper soil is a mixture of four parts loam, with one each of sand, leaf mould, and manure. The pots should be large, and the plants be freely watered. Dust collecting on the foliage injures the beauty and health of this plant, therefore frequent washings are desirable. There are many varieties, some of which, as the snow-ball (*Viburnum opulus*), are hardy shrubs.

HOYA, OR WAX PLANT.

A showy genus of stove climbers, of which one, *Hoya carnosa*, succeeds well with parlor culture. It is a climbing shrub, the leaves dark green and fleshy; the flowers are of a peculiar waxy appearance, produced in umbels, whitish, with rose-colored centre, in which hangs a drop of limpid honey.

Give the plant a large pot, and a compost of peat and loam in equal parts, securing good drainage. Give as much sunlight and heat as possible. The old bloom stalks should not be removed, as they put out flowers year after year. Much water is not needed, especially when the plant is not growing. This beautiful plant is a native of tropical Asia, and is one of the few stove plants that will adapt themselves to parlor culture.

CHRYSANTHEMUMS.

These plants are favorites for autumn blooming, and quite a treatise might be written on their cultivation, since they have become florists' flowers. A few hints must, however, suffice.

The best way to obtain a fine specimen is, to set out in

the garden in the early spring a small plant; give it constant attention during the summer, and pinch out the shoots so as to make lateral branches. About the first of September let it set for bloom, and on the approach of frost, pot it and remove it to the parlor. It will bloom for two months or more. Then dry it off for the winter in the cellar, and by the spring it will furnish you with plenty of young plants. Water should be liberally supplied. The small-flowered, Pompon, varieties are very desirable; the larger flowers are best seen in the garden.

The proper soil is loam and well-rotted manure, with a little silver sand. Waterings of liquid manure are very beneficial as the plants are showing bloom. The following will be found to be fine kinds: —

Pompone.

Andromeda. Cream color.　　*Riquiqui.* Violet plum.
Nellie. Creamy pink.　　*Lady Mayoress.* White.
Miranda. Bright rose.　　*Salamon.* Rosy carmine.
Christiana. Canary yellow.　　*Canary Bird.* Yellow.
Mrs. Dix. Blush.　　*Miss Talford.* White.

Large-Flowered Varieties.

Alarm. Crimson.　　*Prince Albert.* Crimson red.
Little Harry. Golden amber.　　*King of Yellows.* Yellow.
Cassy. Orange and buff.　　*Vesta.* White.
Hermine. Silver white.　　*Annie Salter.* Canary yellow
Pearl. Pearly white.　　*Queen of England.* Blush.

BEGONIA.

The only two species of this ornamental stove plant that do well in the parlor, are *B. incarnata*, and *fuchsioides*. The former is an evergreen shrub, with thick, fleshy stems, and large, drooping clusters of pink flowers in winter. It shows to great advantage if well cared for, and is one of the best window plants. The latter is often called " coral drop," and resembling the former somewhat in habit, produces at all seasons, but chiefly in summer, its pretty, drooping, coral flowers.

Both species require the warmest possible situation, and plenty of light and sun. They are impatient of much water, but the plants should never be allowed to droop. Good drainage is indispensable. The whole family thrive in a compost of one half loam, one half leaf mould, with a slight portion of sand.

CHAPTER VI.

PLANTS FOR WINDOW GARDENING, CONTINUED.

THE SMILAX.

HE plant commonly called smilax is not a true smilax, but a liliaceous plant from the Cape of Good Hope, botanically known as *Myrsiphyllum*, so called from the resemblance of the foliage to that of a myrtle. There are two species — *M. asparagoides*, which is the kind so commonly grown, and *M. angustifolium*. Both species are delicate twining plants, with bright-green foliage (we speak in popular parlance, the parts of these plants usually called leaves being only metamorphosed

branches), and pretty, nodding, fragrant, greenish-white flowers, which are succeeded by bright-red berries.

This plant is easily grown in the parlor, and, twining round the window, makes the prettiest frames imaginable. The root is a bunch of tubers united at the top, from which crown the shoots proceed. Plants may be obtained of any florist in November, and need only a warm, sunny exposure to produce an abundance of foliage. The shoots should be trained on strings, which may be crossed into any required form. The soil should be sandy peat and loam, with good drainage; the pots should be large enough to allow full development of the roots; and, during growth, plenty of water should be given.

About the first of May the plants will go to rest; water should then be gradually withheld, and, when the leaves turn yellow, the plant should be wholly dried off, and remain so all summer, the earth being only just damp enough to prevent the roots from shrivelling up. In October give water, and re-pot the plant. Propagation is effected by division of the root, or from seed, which vegetates freely. The atmosphere of a room in which smilax is grown should be kept rather moist by evaporation of water on the stove or over the furnace, as, in a hot, dry air, the plants are liable to be attacked by red spider, which, as syringing cannot be done in the parlor, are difficult to get rid of.

THE GELSEMIUM.

This plant, botanically *G. sempervirens* or *nitidum*, is commonly known as Carolina jasmine. It is a native of our Southern States, being generally found on the river banks, and along the roads in moist places.

The foliage is dark, shining green; and the flowers, which are freely produced, are bright yellow, and delightfully fragrant.

The soil should be rich sandy loam, and plenty of water should be given when the plant is in growth. Cuttings root easily under a bell-glass.

This is a charming window plant, and easily grown. It is a half climber, and needs the support of a stake or trellis. We have seen a single plant, which, grown in a large tub, occupied the whole of a large bay-window, and was a marked example of what success may be attained in window gardening.

THE STEVIA.

Some species of this large genus are useful as window plants, blooming in early winter, at a time when flowers are scarce.

The foliage is clear green, shining in some species; and the flowers, which are very abundant, are in dense corymbs. The color is usually white, but some are pink or purple.

Cuttings are struck in the spring, grown out of doors all summer, the plants being frequently pinched to keep them in shape. Just before the frost, the plants are potted, shaded for a few days to establish them, and forced into bloom in December. After blooming, the plants are thrown away, except the few needed for cuttings. The soil should be good loam, and water should be given freely. The best species for window culture is *S. salicifolia.*

THE PETUNIA.

This well-known plant blooms freely in the window, and is very easily grown.

It is a native of South America; and from the white

8

variety (*P. nyctiginiflora*) and the small purple (*P. violacea*) all the beautiful varieties now found in gardens have originated.

The plants only require common soil, and to be trained upon a trellis, and, while they give but little bloom in winter, will, towards spring, give the greatest profusion. The double varieties are showy, but are not favorites of ours.

One of the best petunias is Countess of Ellesmere, a charming variety; color rosy-red, with a pure white throat.

FERNS IN THE PARLOR.

Although most ferns can only be grown in the parlor with the protection of a Wardian case, there are some which succeed well grown upon the centre-table, provided the room is light and airy.

We have for years grown some species most successfully in this way, planting them in porcelain pots, or boxes, without drainage from the bottom, in which they have developed finely.

In the bottom of the pot put two layers of potsherds, broken up rather fine, and upon this a few small lumps of charcoal; upon this fill the soil, a compost of peat, loam, and sand, broken fine, but not sifted, and set the plant; give a good watering, and the work is done.

Care must be taken not to over-water so as to rot the roots, and not to keep the room very hot and close.

The species we have found to succeed best in parlor culture are, —

ADIANTUM.

This is a very beautiful and graceful family, of which our native maiden-hair fern is a well-known species.

A. cuneatum. A beautiful Brazilian species, with graceful fronds, which are delicate pink in the young state. It is propagated so readily from spores that young plants often come up in any pots which may be near. If carefully grown, it soon forms a large plant.

A. affine. A delicate species from New Zealand, very easily grown.

A. pedatum. Our native maiden-hair.

A. capillus Veneris. The English maiden-hair.

Both of very easy culture.

DAVILLIA.

D. canariensis. A graceful and pretty fern. Does well with parlor culture.

BLECHNUM.

B. braziliense is a large-growing, rather coarse, but handsome fern, which makes a good specimen with room culture.

PTERIS.

Of this large family three are easily grown in the parlor, and probably experiment would show that many others succeed equally well.

P. serrulata. This is the most common of exotic ferns. A native of the East Indies, it comes up from spores so readily, in fern and orchid houses, as to become a weed. It grows rapidly, and soon makes a large plant.

P. tremula. A large-growing species, from Australia. It makes a fine plant for an ornamental porcelain pot, or for a low-hanging basket.

P. cretica albo lineata. A pretty fern, and the only one of the variegated kinds which will thrive with parlor culture. The leaves are light green, with a clear-white centre and midrib. It is now very common.

NEPHROLEPIS.

N. exaltata and *pectinata* are common kinds, easily grown and very ornamental.

POLYPODIUM.

Those who cannot obtain exotic ferns may cultivate successfully our pretty, wild polypodium (*P. vulgare*). It is
an evergreen species, very common on shaded, rocky
places, and grows well in the parlor.

LYGODIUM.

This is a beautiful genus of climbing ferns, of which one
species (*L. palmatum*) is not uncommon in New England.

The oldest known species is *L. scandens*, a native of
the East Indies, with large, bright-green foliage, and which,
grown upon the rafters of a greenhouse, makes a screen of
delicate beauty. It does well in a Wardian case, but is
impatient of damp, unless in a high temperature.

L. japonicum is a charming little climber, and will
thrive in a Wardian case, or even in the parlor, if the air
is not allowed to get very dry.

L. palmatum (our "climbing-fern ") is hardy and easily
cultivated.

CHRYSANTHEMUMS.

The recently introduced Japanese chrysanthemums are
valuable as prolonging the season of flowers far into the

winter, although the flowers are very ragged and loose. The best way for the amateur is to buy from the nearest green-house a few plants of chrysanthemums in the autumn, bloom them in the window, and then throw them away.

AGAVE, OR CENTURY PLANT.

The common Century plant, or American aloe (*A. Americana*), and the striped-leaved variety, are too well known to need description. They are very hardy plants, even bearing several degrees of frost without injury. They are stately plants, and will endure much ill-treatment. In the parlor they form attractive ornaments for the centre-table in winter, the only care required being not to over-water them, and to dust the leaves.

There are many other species, all worth growing; but the best are, —

A. Milleri. A variety of *Americana*, of free-growing habit, and with long variegated leaves.

A. a medio picta. Rich golden-yellow leaves.

A. applanata. Rich glaucous foliage.

A. coccinia. A massive species; deep green leaves, armed with red spines.

A. ferox. A very distinct species, with heavy dark-green leaves, armed with large dark-brown spines.

A. filifera. Leaves dark green, clothed with white filaments. A very handsome plant.

A. Ghiesbreghtii. A very distinct species. Leaves bright green, bordered with red, and armed with red spines.

A. Schedigera. A handsome plant, resembling *A. filifera*, but much more beautiful. The edges of the leaves are white, and from these hang long woolly filaments.

A. univittata. Leaves dark green, with central stripe of greenish yellow.

A. Verschaffeltii. A showy species. Foliage milky green, with large brown spines.

A. Xalapensis. A beautiful plant. Leaves dark clear green, the edges thickly set with rich brown spines.

A. xylacantha. Leaves glaucous green, with broad white margin.

There are scores of other species and varieties, all handsome and well worth growing, all evergreen except *A. virginiana*, which is deciduous.

GERANIUMS, OR PELARGONIUMS.

The past few years have witnessed a rapid advance in these plants. Great improvements have been made in both foliage and flower — in the former, by more vivid and better defined markings; in the latter, in size, shape, substance, and color. Some of the new varieties have foliage which equals in color a brilliant flower, and in some the permanency of the markings is most remarkable.

Of thousands of varieties we select the following as the best for parlor culture, both as regards foliage and profusion of bloom : —

Duchess. Salmon scarlet.　　　　*Maid of Kent*. Pink.
General Grant. Scarlet. Large.　*Madam Vaucher*. White.
Orbiculatum. 　　" 　　Dwarf.　*Crystal Palace Gem*. Variegated.
Louis Veuillot. 　" 　　　　　　Gold.
Warrior. 　　　" 　　　　　*Mountain of Snow*. Variegated.
Cybister. 　　　" 　　　　　　Silver.
Gloire de Corbenay. Salmon.　　*Mrs. Pollock*. Variegated. Bronze.
Gertrude (Barker's). Salmon pink.　*Lady Cullum*. 　" 　　"
Helen Lindsay. Pink.

DOUBLE GERANIUMS.

These varieties are not very free-blooming in the parlor, and are better adapted for the green-house. However, after the turn of the year, they often produce good flowers, and are then very showy, the blossoms remaining long in perfection. They need a rich soil and plenty of water, as they are generally strong growers, although plants bloom when very young.

The best are, —

Gloire de Nancy. Double. Cherry.
William Pitt. 　　　" 　　Scarlet.
Madam Lemoine. 　" 　　Pink.
Marie Lemoine. 　　" 　　"

It is said a double white variety has been produced in France; but if so, it is not yet for sale in this country.

Ivy-leaved Geraniums.

The old ivy-leaved geranium (*P. peltatum*) is a well-known window plant, of easy culture. The leaf is ornamental, and the flower, though not very showy, is pretty. This species has been wonderfully improved during the past few years.

A variety with leaves beautifully marked with silver has been raised, which proves a capital window plant, and requires no more care than the old kind. There is also a variety with golden-edged leaves.

There has also been great improvement in the flower. The first advance in this direction was *P. peltatum elegans*, in which the flowers were bright pink, and of better form. Next we had Princess Thyra, flowers deep flesh color, marked with pink; and Grand Duchess Maria, violet pink, with deep violet marks. But the latest and by far the finest varieties are those with bright rosy-pink or scarlet blossoms, which are so beautiful that, when they become common, they must be favorite window plants. They are hybrids between the zonale and ivy-leaved sections, but retain the ivy leaf while gaining the brilliancy of flower of the zonale varieties. *Willsii* has deep scarlet blossoms; and in *Willsii rosea* they are delicate salmon rose. Lady Edith and Gem of the Season are two of the newest varieties, which are superior to all others in color and form of flower.

PALMS FOR HOUSE CULTURE.

Many of the palms are very ornamental grown in the parlor. Their stiff foliage is well adapted to endure the impure air of apartments, and is not injured by gas. They also thrive with very little sun, and are easily kept clean by dusting or washing. It is, however, only the more hardy species which can be so used, and the best of all is fortunately the most common.

Livistona bourbonica, commonly known as *Latania bourbonica*, is a showy plant, with broad fan-shaped leaves, which grows freely, and is very useful for interior decoration. All the species of *Chamœrops* are very hardy, and are very easily grown. The most common are *C. humilis*, *Fortunei*, and *Palmetto*.

Corypha australis is a noble plant, and of easy culture. All the *Cycas* are hardy enough to do well in the parlor. But by far the most beautiful is *Seaforthia elegans*, a very graceful plant.

Where plants are needed for effect, and little attention can be given, palms and agaves are eminently useful. All winter they need little care, and, provided they are well grown in summer, will only from November to April require an occasional watering; in fact, the care to give is, to see they are not over-watered. Of course we cannot give full descriptions of all; but, as a general rule, any green-house palm will thrive in the parlor, and well repay the little care it needs.

CHAPTER VII.

HANGING BASKETS AND SUITABLE PLANTS, AND TREAT-
MENT OF IVY.

HAT a pretty amusement is the growth
of plants in hanging baskets or
pots! It is very popular, and
deservedly so. The beauty of
the baskets, now fashioned in so
many artistic designs, is almost
sufficient to inspire a love of hor-
ticulture, if only for the sake
of growing the plant in so
pretty a pot. Yet we cannot urge
the growth of plants in these baskets; a porous pot is essential to
the health of a plant, and most of
these baskets are china, or glazed or painted.

Yet they may be used by setting the pot containing the

plant inside of them.   Another objection is, that having no outlet for the escape of the water, it collects in the bottom, and, unless there is very ample drainage, which is seldom the case, the roots are rotting in water while the surface is dry.

Potting in these vases is very simple.   If the plant must be in the vase or basket, fill half full of broken potsherds; on these place a thin layer of moss, and fill up with prepared soil; shade the plant for a few days until well established, then hang it in the window, and water slightly every morning with a fine-rosed watering-pot; as the plant grows, dispose the branches to fall gracefully over the pot.

The plants most suitable for baskets are, —

The COMMON PERIWINKLE (Vinca Major and Minor), and the pretty variety with variegated leaves.   This is an evergreen, and produces its pretty blue flowers in spring and early summer.   There is also a white-flowered and a double variety.

LYSIMACHIA MUMMULARIA (Money Wort).   A pretty little trailing plant, with dark, glossy leaves, and a profusion of dark yellow flowers in June.   This plant should be in a shady window.

LINARIA CYMBALARIA (Coliseum Ivy).   A little gem

of a plant, and thriving well in the parlor. Leaves small; ivy-shaped flowers, like a little snap-dragon, purple and white. Should be kept rather moist.

TRADESCANTIA ZEBRINA. A rapid growing plant, with greenish purple leaves, with lighter markings on the upper side, and dark purple below; flowers small light pink.

CEREUS FLAGELLIFORMIS. — A pretty species of cactus, with pink flowers in summer, and long, pendulous leaves, with close spines.

LOBELIA GRACILIS AND ERINUS. These, and many others of the family, are pretty, graceful plants, producing blue or white flowers. Sow the seed in early spring, and plants will bloom in June, and continue in blossom all summer.

NEMOPHILA. A class of pretty annuals, with blue, white, and spotted flowers. Treat as lobelia.

TROPÆOLUM (Nasturtium). The various small-flowered kinds do well, and are gay with flowers, if the pot is large enough, and the soil not too rich.

SOLANUM JASMINOIDES. This pretty plant, previously described, does well in a large basket.

SAXIFRAGA SARMENTOSA (Chinese Saxifrage). Very

pretty and common, producing long, hanging runners, with new plants growing out every few inches. The flower is white, produced on a tall spike, from the centre of the old plant. It is not showy, and the bud, when young, should be cut off, as the plant dies after blooming. Give plenty of water.

CONVOLVULUS MAURITANICUS. A beautiful, new Morning Glory, with pink and blue flowers, with a white star in the centre.

PELARGONIUM LATERIPES (Ivy-leaved Geranium). Makes an excellent plant for a basket, and will do well with little care; the variegated-leaved variety is very fine.

DISANDRA PROSTRATA. A pretty, free-growing plant, with long, slender stems, clothed with roundish leaves, and bearing small, yellow flowers, of no particular beauty; cultivated more for its freedom of growth than for its flowers. Grows in any light, loamy soil.

One of the most serviceable trailers is the plant commonly known as German Ivy (*Senecio Scandens*); it is of most rapid growth, with light green leaves, studded with pellucid dots, and never troubled by insects. As a screen for a window, or covering for a wall, it is most valuable. It is easily propagated, every joint rooting if placed in the earth. The flowers are straw-colored, and often produced in greatest profusion. The plant is a native of the Cape of Good Hope, and has been introduced many years. It is admirably adapted for baskets.

IVY.

This plant, in some of its varieties, is probably the most popular ornament of the parlor. The ease of culture, its beautiful foliage, its rapid growth, and evergreen character, all combine to make it a favorite.

The soil should be a rich loam; the richer the soil the more rapid will be the growth. Yet avoid stimulating manures.

Slips root readily, taken off at any leaf joint, and placed either in earth or water; in the latter they will soon throw out roots, and may then be transferred to pots.

The only precaution to be taken in growing ivy is to keep it from frost while in growth; and if frozen, to keep the sun away from it, thawing it out with cold water.

In summer the plants may be set out of doors, and will make vigorous growth.

There are many species, of which the most common is

Hedera Helix, the common twining ivy, a native of Europe, of which there are many varieties. The leaves of these varieties vary very much, and many distinctions have been founded on these variations. There are two very beautiful kinds, the silver and golden, the foliage being beautifully variegated with white and gold. The following cuts will

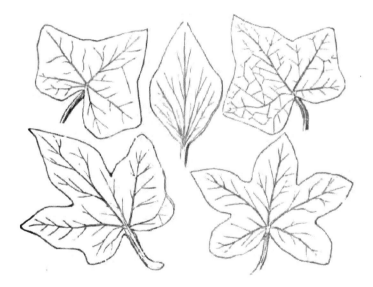

show how these differ in foliage, all being taken from living leaves, though some are necessarily reduced in size to accommodate them to our pages.

The Tree or Aborescent Ivy is merely a form of the com-

9

mon variety, which is shown by its returning to the primal form not unfrequently. The leaves are entire, and the plant often retains its arborescent form for years.

H. Rœgneriana is a variety with large, heart-shaped leaves, which is much esteemed.

H. h. digitata, the palmate or hand-shaped Ivy is a

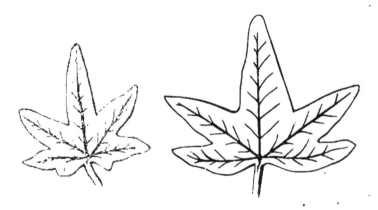

pretty variety, of rapid growth; the leaves are small, dark, and veined. This is often called, erroneously, the Irish Ivy.

H. Canariensis is the Irish, or Giant Ivy; the leaves are five-lobed, and larger than those of the common ivy.

Almost all the varieties of nurserymens' catalogues are merely forms of these, with peculiar foliage.

The Golden Ivy is a splendid plant; when the young leaves come out it resembles a mass of yellow flowers.

Ivies are grown in hanging baskets, around windows, made to trail around picture frames and looking glasses; indeed, they may be made decorative in the highest degree.

The plants should always be well supplied with water, though it should never be allowed to stand at the roots. Large plants of the common varieties may be procured for fifty cents. The ornamental foliaged varieties are somewhat dearer.

If you have ivy growing out of doors (and it will thrive if you keep the winter's sun away from it), a pretty effect may be produced by cutting large branches, and keeping them in vases of rain water. They will grow well all winter, and planted in spring make nice plants for autumn.

The plant commonly known as German Ivy is not an ivy; the botanical name is *Senecio Scandens*. It is deservedly popular, from its rapid growth and its freedom from insects. We have, in a former paragraph, treated of it more fully.

The Coliseum Ivy is a species of Snap-dragon, as may be seen from an examination of the flowers, and a very pretty plant it is; botanically it is *Linaria Cymbalaria*, and is mentioned more fully in the early part of this chapter.

Five-leaved Ivy is the Virginia Creeper or Woodbine (*Ampelopsis Virginica*), a native of our woods.

The Poison Ivy is *Rhus Radicans* or *Rhus Toxicoden-dron*, and not of the same family as any of the above.

CHAPTER VIII.

PLANTS FOR WINDOW GARDENING, CONTINUED.

ABUTILON : New Varieties. CALLA LILY : Growth in Cases in the Window. OXALIS : Description. — Soil. — Species. CUPHEA HYSSOPIFOLIA. CHRYSANTHEMUM : New Varieties. LILY OF THE VALLEY : Forcing in House Culture.

THE ABUTILON.

THE past few years have given us some new varieties of Abutilon which are very valuable as window plants.

As we have before remarked, all the Abutilons are of very easy culture, thrive well in the close, dry atmosphere of the house, flower freely, and are not liable to the attacks of insects, and in all these good qualities the new varieties are in no respect inferior to the old.

Abutilon vexillarium is a charming, small-leaved species, of which the variety with the foliage beautifully marked with gold is most common in cultivation. The habit of the plant is trailing, the shoots weak and drooping, which fits it for carpet bedding in the garden, or for window culture in hanging baskets.

Grafted on a tall stem of one of the tall-growing species it forms a beautiful head of pendulous sprays, and is a very handsome plant. The flowers are bright yellow from a red calyx, and with protruding black pistil, and from the peculiar combination of rich colors, are very effective.

The plant is now common, and may be obtained at any green-house.

Cuttings root freely on sandy loam.

Abutilon Verschaffeltii is a tall growing species with woolly leaves and light-yellow flowers. It blooms freely when very young, and is seldom out of flower. It is a rapid grower and a very attractive plant. In the summer it makes a fine show in the garden. As in most of the species, the flowers are pendulous on long footstalks.

Abutilon Boule de Neige is a new seedling of French origin. As a decorative free blooming plant it is unsurpassed, plants only a few inches high blooming freely. The blossoms are large, pure, lustrous white, with bright yellow pistil, the contrast of color adding greatly to the effect. Although a new plant, it increases so readily that it is easily obtainable; superior in every respect, it is one of the greatest acquisitions of the last few years.

CALLA LILY.

This plant can be very prettily grown in a window, in hollow tables.

These should be made as long as the window, and about two feet wide. The bulb tables now in general use do very well if made a little deeper, for the Calla requires plenty of root-room.

A zinc pan is set into the table; in this the pots are placed, and all interstices are filled with moss; a covering of green moss is then placed over all, and we have the lilies springing from a bed of moss. Water very freely, even to filling the pan half full, and give all the light and sun possible, occasionally turning the table, as the plants grow to the window. The amount of bloom to be obtained from a dozen good sized Callas treated in this way is surprising; from November to May there will seldom be less than an average of one flower to a plant.

In May, take the plants out of the pots and plant them in rich, deep soil out of doors; the foliage will die down and the root go to rest. About August it will begin to grow again, and the plants will be ready for potting by the middle of September.

Thus treated, Callas bloom far more vigorously than when kept growing all the year.

There is a new dwarf Calla which is very pretty and desirable where economy of room is an object, but it is not as showy as the old kind.

The Spotted-leaved Calla (*Richardia albo maculata*) is valuable for its spotted arrow-shaped foliage; the flower is green and not showy: the plant dies down after blooming, and must then be dried off.

OXALIS.

There are about a hundred species of these pretty bulbs, some of which grow and bloom well in the window.

The foliage is generally petiolate, and much resembles clover. The flowers are mostly yellow, pink, red, or white, and the various shades of these colors, and are often fragrant.

They open in the sun, closing in dull weather and at night.

Many are free bloomers, and all are remarkably clean plants, seldom being infested with insects.

All are of low habit, and some are well adapted for hanging baskets.

The bulbs should be potted, half a dozen in an eight-inch pot, — or better, a dozen in a twelve-inch pan, — in sandy loam, with good drainage, about the first of October.

The foliage will soon appear, in some species with flowers, but generally the foliage will grow for a month before bloom begins.

After blooming, grow the foliage well, giving plenty of water until it begins to turn yellow, then gradually reduce the supply of water and put the pots on a closet shelf, letting them remain without water until the next autumn.

Some of the best varieties are

O. Boweii, flowers bright rosy red, very large, from October.

O. cernua, a common species with a double variety ; flowers bright yellow, very fragrant, all winter.

O. versicolor, a charming plant with fine-cut foliage, the flowers outside crimson red, inside creamy white.   This species grows best in a hanging basket.

O. luxula and the variety *alba* are beautiful plants, the foliage is in tufts, the flowers on long footstalks standing well above it.   They are very large, rosy pink or white, with yellow centre.

A table of Oxalis every year fills for us a sunny window,

and all through the long days of winter it is gay with bright blossoms, and gives quite as much pleasure as the rare exotics which are brought from the greenhouse.

CUPHEA.

A new Cuphea (*C. hyssopifolia*) has proved a very free blooming plant, being never out of bloom. The foliage is dark green, very fine; the flowers bright pink, completely covering the plant. It roots freely from cuttings, grows rapidly; the plants bloom when only an inch high, and whether in garden, greenhouse, or window, it devotes its whole energies to flowering.

Soil, sandy loam, with good drainage.

CHRYSANTHEMUM.

LARGE FLOWERED.

Some of the best new varieties are—

George Peabody, pure white.

Gloria Mundi, golden yellow, incurved.

Princess of Teck, pure white, finely incurved.

Marchioness of Lorne, rich rosy lilac.

Bijou, bright rose purple, anemone flowered.

Jardin des Plants, golden yellow.

Margaret, large pure white, anemone flowered.

POMPONE.

Andromeda rosea, fine rose.

Bob, rich deep crimson.

Carminata, crimson-red.

Fabeola, lilac, anemone-flowered.

Reine des Anemones, white, anemone-flowered.

Embleme, pure yellow.

Brilliant, orange-red.

Model of Perfection, rich lilac.

Madam Eugene Domage, pure white.

Rose d'amour, clear rose.

The Japanese varieties with tasselled flowers are more curious than beautiful. Some good kinds are *Acquisition, Beaumont, Elaine, Jane Salter, La Coquette, Garnet, L'Ornament de la Nature.*

LILY OF THE VALLEY.

Forcing this plant for winter bloom has latterly become quite a business with florists; but it is not generally known that in a dwelling-house fine winter flowers can be had with very little trouble.

The pips or clumps of roots can be obtained from any

dealer in bulbs in October. Put them at once in good garden soil, placing them thick in the pot.

Water moderately, and place the pots in a shed where they will freeze. About the first of January bring the pots into the kitchen, and place them on the shelf over the range, or in any very warm place, giving plenty of water.

The leaves and flower-stalks will rapidly develop, but will be without color. When they are sufficiently long, bring them into full sunlight, where they will get color in a very short time. Some of the best flowers we have ever seen were grown in this way.

Surely the beauty and fragrance of this favorite flower will repay any trouble. We should never weary of the Lily of the Valley, could we gather it every day in the year.

CHAPTER IX.

ORCHIDS FOR PARLOR CULTURE.

LYCASTE. — ODONTOGLOSSUM. — CYPRIPEDIUM. — BLETIA. — PHAIUS. — GOODYERA.

THE word "orchid" conveys to most minds an idea of a plant which grows only in great heat, and requires a peculiar mode of culture. To some, "orchid" is synonymous with air plant; yet a large portion of orchids are not air plants (epiphytal), and many thrive in a moderate temperature, and require no peculiar culture.

Some orchids grow at such elevation that hoar-frost is found upon the leaves, while others are natives of the hot jungles of the Indian Archipelago.

Formerly all orchids were grown in a hot, steamy atmosphere, that being the treatment which theory recommended. The natural consequence was that many perished under such uncongenial culture.

The past few years have shown that orchids from cool regions require cool culture, a temperature somewhat resembling that of their native haunts. The only wonder is that horticulturists were thirty years in opening their eyes to this patent fact.

Experience has also shown that some few of the large class of cool orchids can be successfully grown and bloomed in the parlor.

Many orchids are remarkable only for their showy flowers, the foliage being sparse or deciduous. But those orchids adapted to parlor culture are all from genera having evergreen leaves, and the foliage of some is ornamental.

The general rules for potting orchids are : Give plenty of drainage — no orchids thrive in a close, sour soil, many require plenty of water, but none thrive in standing water ; make the soil porous, lumpy, — broken, not sifted ; give pure air and light, and a decided season of rest ; keep the foliage clean and free from dust, and preserve the roots from their numerous insect enemies.

LYCASTE.

A family of some thirty species of terrestrial orchids from South America.

The leaves are large and plaited, the flowers borne usually on single scapes, large and very showy.

These plants should be potted in coarse peat and sphagnum moss, with broken potsherds or bits of charcoal.

When growing they need plenty of water, and even when at rest should never be allowed to become entirely dry.

L. Skinneri. This beautiful plant is a native of Guatemala. The flowers are large, from three to six inches in diameter, sepals and petals white or rose, recurved, lip varying from pure white to deepest carmine. The growth is made in summer, the flowers are produced in winter; they last six weeks in beauty, and many are produced in succession.

Although a close, moist atmosphere is best suited to this plant when in growth, it may be grown in the parlor. Give plenty of water and light without full sun, the object being to grow the foliage as large as possible. When growth is complete, generally by October, reduce the water and give more sun.

Those who have a vinery can grow this plant in great perfection; put them in the vinery from May to October, in the parlor from October to May. Figured in Bot. Mag., tab. 4445. Pax. Mag., 11, p. 1.

L. Harrisoniæ. A showy species which is easily grown in the parlor. The leaf is large and solitary, the flowers three inches in diameter, one or two on a spike, white or yellowish, waxy, lip rich rose, varying to lilac. This plant blooms constantly at all seasons. Bot. Reg., tab. 897.

ODONTOGLOSSUM.

A large genus of generally cool orchids. Doubtless many of these beautiful plants could be grown in the parlor; we have, however, had experience with only one.

O. grande. A noble species, with dark evergreen foliage. Flowers on erect racemes, five inches across; glossy yellow, beautifully barred with chocolate; produced freely in autumn and early winter.

Pot in sphagnum moss, coarse peat, and charcoal.

Treated as prescribed for *Lycaste Skinneri* it blooms freely.

CYPRIPEDIUM.

A very large genus, inhabiting in some species both continents, both in the temperate and torrid zones. The plants are commonly known as Lady's Slipper. We have in our woods beautiful species, and among exotics many no less attractive.

Our native species, if potted late in the autumn, will bloom in the window in early spring.

The best species for parlor culture is —·

C. insigne. A noble plant from Nepal; foliage narrow, dark green; flower solitary (rarely two), three inches broad, greenish edged with white; wings long, purple and yellow. The flowers are very freely produced from November to February, and last two months in perfection.

We have now (January, 1876) a plant in the parlor window, with thirty-six flowers, which has been in full beauty for four weeks; the pot is two feet in diameter, and this plant has been grown from a single small pot in two years. This, however, was in the greenhouse; but in the parlor the growth, though slower, is no less satisfactory.

Soil, rich peaty loam. This plant should never be allowed to get dry, and requires very little rest. Grow in full sunshine.

C. venustum. A pretty species, with beautiful, variegated foliage; flowers, rich brown, green, and chocolate, but not very showy.

Requires the same soil and general treatment as the last.

BLETIA.

A family of terrestrial orchids of easy culture. The root-stocks should be potted in autumn, grown with plenty of sun and water. The flowers are produced in March on terminal spikes, and though transient, are very pretty.

Soil, rich loam. After blooming, the foliage dies away and the roots go to rest.

B. hyacinthina. A delicate species, with purple flowers, marked with white, somewhat resembling our wild *Calopogon.* Easily grown.

PHAIUS.

These plants are tall growers, with large broad evergreen foliage, and tall scapes of large handsome flowers.

They need a rich soil, plenty of water, and full light and sun-heat.

P. grandifolius, a native of China, grows and flowers well in the parlor. Although an orchid it will stand more hard usage than most plants. The flowers are white externally, purplish brown inside, lip white and brown. Blooms freely from January to March. A more showy plant, both in growth and flower, it would be hard to find. We have grown plants, with forty scapes carrying more than five hundred flowers.

GOODYERA.

Pretty terrestrial orchids, of which two species, natives of shady woods, are very pretty parlor plants.

G. pubescens and *repens* are not rare plants, but if potted in rich leaf mould they are very showy in window culture. The foliage is green, with silver tracery; the flowers white, in erect spikes.

Many rare exotics possess less beauty than these simple native plants.

CHAPTER X.

ROMAN HYACINTHS: forcing for Christmas. SUCCULENTS as Window Plants.—
HARDY AND HALF HARDY EVERGREENS: Hall and Vestibule Decoration. HOL-
LIES.—RETINOSPORA.—YUCCAS.—TAXUS.—THUJA.—CUPRESSUS.—THUJOPSIS.—
Propagation of Evergreens by Window Culture.

THE Roman Hyacinth is a charming early blooming
species admirably adapted for forcing, and easily
grown in the parlor. It is the earliest autumn-flowering
bulb we have, and by potting for succession may be had in
bloom from November to March.

Each bulb gives from one to four spikes of pure white
deliciously fragrant flowers.

They are best grown in large flat pans, and the bulbs,
which are small, should be planted about an inch apart each
way.

The soil should be sandy loam, and the plants should be
well grown, freely watered, and occasionally with liquid
manure. This plant has been long in cultivation, having
been introduced in 1596.

To have this plant in bloom for Christmas, when it is particularly valuable on account of the scarcity of pure white flowers at that season, we should pot the bulbs the latter part of September; set the pots in a dark place, watering moderately for about three weeks. The pots will then be full of roots, and the plants may be set in the window; the shoots will grow rapidly and soon show flowers.

Botanically this plant is *Bellevalia operculata*, sometimes *Hyacinthus romanus*.

Bulbs cost about six dollars a hundred.

SUCCULENTS.

The plants known as Succulents comprise many genera varying much in appearance, but all requiring the same general culture. The soil should be porous, well drained, and sandy loam. The pots should generally be small, as a majority of these plants are low, flat growers. Great care should be used in watering, lest an excess make the plant rot off.

With few exception, these plants are valuable only for their neat and attractive growth or for beautiful foliage; some however are very beautiful in flower.

At present these plants are very popular, and many fine collections exist, numbering many hundreds of species.

A window full of neatly potted plants of *Sempervivum*, *Haworthia*, *Echeveria*, *Aloe*, *Rhipsalis*, *Crassula*, or in fact of any of the many genera, is very attractive. Our space allows us to mention but very few.

All the Sempervivums, from the common House-leek (*S. tectorum*), are very interesting; the neat rosette plants are beautiful and the flowers curious.

The Echiverias are showy in foliage, and one variety *E. lutea grandiflora*, is a free blooming and very handsome plant. *E. rosacea* or *mexicana* is a glaucous green and forms a perfect rosette.

Crassula perfoliata is an admirable window plant. The flowers are pure white, in loose spikes, and are freely produced about Christmas.

Pachyphytum bracteosum has thick fleshy leaves, covered with silvery bloom.

It is a very beautiful plant.

Othonna crassifolia has light yellowish-green fleshy foliage and bright yellow flowers. For a hanging basket, it is invaluable, and in the garden it forms the best carpet for bedding.

All the Century Plants (Agave) and Aloes are suitable for window culture, although they are generally of large growth. They are however easily grown, require little care, and are exceedingly ornamental.

HARDY AND HALF-HARDY EVERGREENS.

Many of these are of low growth, and are suitable for hall or vestibule decoration. They only require to be lifted from the garden late in the autumn, and to be potted in common loam.

During the winter they will not grow, so they need but little water, — in fact the soil should be kept moist, but never wet ; the only other care they will require is frequent dusting of the foliage with a feather duster.

In spring the plants may be planted out in the garden for summer growth.

Some of the best plants for this mode of decoration are—

HOLLIES.

These plants are not thoroughly hardy in New England, but for summer decoration they are very fine.

Some of the best varieties are —

Common Green Holly (*Ilex aquifolium*), in its many varieties, *I. ferox, myrtifolia, laurifolia, scottica, serratifolia, angustifolia*, and others.

The Variegated Hollies: Golden Queen and Silver Queen.

All these can be imported, trained as bushes, pyramids, or trees; and whether in foliage or also covered with the bright scarlet berries, are very ornamental.

The American Holly (*Ilex opaca*) is hardy.

RETINOSPORA.

These are among the most beautiful of evergreens; neat in growth, attractive in appearance, dwarf, compact, and often delicate and graceful in foliage, they possess all good qualities.

Some of the best are *R. ericoides*, glaucous green with purple tinge; *filifera*, long slender branches; *lycopodioides*, very delicate; the variegated varieties of *obtusa*; and *pisifera*, all beautiful, and the showy *plumosa*.

YUCCAS.

These showy plants are adapted for hall decoration.

The best are *Y. recurvata, gloriosa, aloefolia,* and the variegated kinds.

These are half-hardy; the more tender species need greenhouse culture.

Taxus.

The Golden Yew (*T. baccatta aurea*) is a very handsome plant, bright in color, and very desirable.

T. elegantissima is far brighter and better.

T. fastigiata is the Irish yew ; a very erect grower, suit-able for tubs on each side of a vestibule.

Thuja.

Many of the tender Arbor Vitæs are very handsome, grown as specimens.

The best are *T. aurea* and *T. semper aurea*, the latter of which retains its golden foliage throughout the year.

Cupressus.

The cypress is not hardy with us, but is valuable for the garden in summer and the hall in winter.

The best is *C. Lawsoniana* in its many forms; pendulous, variegated gold and silver, dwarf, and the magnificent fasti-gate variety, *C. erecta viridis.*

All are beautiful, and the number to be grown is only to be limited by the winter accommodation and the length of our purses.

THUJOPSIS.

T. vorialis is a showy plant, not thoroughly hardy in New England, though often surviving uninjured by the winter.

It is of a bright lively green, of elegant growth, and resembles a cross between a cypress and an arbor vitæ.

PROPAGATION BY WINDOW CULTURE.

A very easy way to get a stock of young evergreens, and at the same time to have a pretty show in a window, is to take off the tips of the shoots of such varieties as we wish to increase, in November.

Fill some long boxes which fit the window with pure fresh white sand, level the surface, give a good watering, and then plant the tips in close lines till the boxes are filled.

If we have the variegated kinds, the effect is very pretty.

Keep the sand just wet, do not allow the plants to freeze, but keep them cool; give plenty of light but no hot sun.

This little window-garden will be very attractive, and by spring many of the cuttings will have good roots, when they may be planted out.

Printed in the USA
CPSIA information can be obtained
at www.ICGtesting.com
LVHW051034190224
772231LV00003B/36